An Illustrated History of the

BARREL

in America

Jack L. Shagena, P. E. (Ret.)

Copyright © 2006
Jack L. Shagena, Jr.
All rights reserved

Privately Printed by the Author

Printing 1 2 3 4 5 6 7 8 9 10

January 2006 – 500 copies

For Copies:

Jack L. Shagena, Jr.
2017 Gumtree Terrace
Bel Air, Maryland 21015

Tel: 410-569-0988
jshagena@comcast.net

Library of Congress Control Number: 2005911068

ISBN 0-9776866-0-4

Printed in the U. S. A.
InstantPublisher.com

Best regards,
Jack Shoejevn
2006

An enterprising lad purchased barrels of potash from a country store and transported them downriver to Boston. With the proceeds from the sale he bought notions that were sold at the rural store. From *Wide Awake*, 1882.

The stamp on the back cover depicting a rural post office and country store was issued September 27, 1972 to celebrate the 100th Anniversary of Mail Order.

Preface

The unsung, almost forgotten, and practically unnoticed commerce container for more than two millenniums is still around and virtually unchanged. Early barrels were so well designed that almost no modifications have evolved in their construction for hundreds of years – a remarkable occurrence in the history of mechanical structures.

The many centuries of utility and endurance for these wooden containers is primarily attributed to the barrel's robustness created by the sturdy double-arch principle. Today, however, the barrel endures for culinary reasons in the ageing and seasoning of distilled liquors, wines, sauces, and vinegars. Plastic and metal containers are cheaper, and in some cases longer lasting, but do not produce sipping alcoholic beverages and condiments with acceptable qualities to the discerning consumer.

Per British tradition, wooden containers are called casks and were produced in America by coopers who immigrated during the seventeenth and eighteenth centuries. Originally only a specific size of a cask was designated a barrel, but as the craft developed in the United States, *barrel* became the accepted name for most casks, *hogsheads* for very large ones holding tobacco, and *kegs* for the smaller containers.

This book begins with a short history of the barrel in ancient times, and then addresses the container's development in early America, how it was made, and how, over the years with increasing production, its name became inevitably woven into the written and spoken fabric of the American language. Expression such as "cash on the barrel head," and "a bad apple spoils the barrel;" as well as *barrel-speak,* with such terms as barrel house, barrel organ, and barreling along are presented, illustrated, and discussed.

Today, cardboard boxes and the more durable and lower cost fifty-five gallon drum has largely replaced the wooden barrel as the shipping container of choice. A hammered end section of the metal container has attained a place in our culture as a Jamaican steel drum, but this musical instrument has not overshadowed the robust wooden barrel that seems to roll on forever.

This effort evolved out of a study of eighteenth century gristmills that produced flour, which was shipped to many corners of the world in barrels. By the early part of the twentieth century, cotton and paper sacks replaced the barrels, however, the it's odd that little information existed on the barrel, which was also used to transport most bulk agricultural and mining products. An investigation uncovered scattered information about the ubiquitous but virtually ignored wooden container that facilitated commerce; and with the exception of bundled barrel staves, head and hoops, called *shooks*, little has been documented to celebrate the importance of barrels and the contributions of those hardy coopers who produced them.

Three-dimensional mechanical devices like the barrel are best understood with illustrations that show how they are constructed, moved about warehouses, and transported. Therefore, this history is profusely illustrated with many old line drawings, a number of new ones, and a few photographs.

Words and pictures, however, cannot adequately substitute for the smell of newly shaven wood, the aroma of the barrel being heated over a fire to bend the staves, and the lusty clamor of the cooperage shop producing barrels. For the most part, these sensations are gone forever, but otherwise the barrel story can be vividly revisited and relived for today's reader.

Jack L. Shagena, Jr.
Bel Air, Maryland
November 2005

Contents

Preface	3
Chapter 1 – Early History of the Wooden Container	11
Egyptian Straight-sided Tub	15
Egyptian Tapered Tub	16
Palm Tree Cask	17
Alpine Valley Cask	17
Cask Are Prevalent and The American Barrel	18
Was the Barrel Invented?	20
Chapter 2 – The Robust Barrel: Handle with Care?	27
Description of the Barrel	27
Robustness Examined	28
The Pre-stressed Barrel	29
The Wheel Comparison	32
Speculation on the Barrel Shape	34
Over Niagara Falls	35
Handle with Care?	39
Removing the Bung	42
Re-coopering	43
Chapter 3 – The Barrel in Colonial America	45
Stave Exportation	46
Tobacco	47
Naval Stores	52
Beef and Pork	53
Molasses and Rum	54
Apple Cider	55
Cod Fishing	57
Whale Oil	59
Wheat and Flour	60
Trade with Native Americans	61

Revolutionary War 62
Domestic Woodenware 63

Chapter 4 – Making an American Barrel 67

Types of Cooperage 67
The Cooper's *Block* 69
Stave Blanks or Billets 70
Listing the Stave 72
Putting the S*hot* on the Stave 75
Raising the Barrel 77
Preparing the "Case" for the Heads 80
Making the Barrelheads 82
"Cleaning Down" 84
Installing the Heads and Hoops 85
Clothing and Tools 87
Summary 88

Chapter 5 – America Barrels Along 89

The Embargo Act 90
A Canal and the *Constellation* 94
Railroads 95
Oil Gushes in Pennsylvania 96
Civil War Intervenes 100
Barrel Machinery Improves 104
The Cooper Fights Back 107
Flour Barrels 109
Beer Barrels 111
Whiskey Barrels 112
Government Standardization 114
The King of Packages 115
Barrels Contained Everything 117

Chapter 6 – Those Inventive Americans 121

Assessable Heads 121
Moving Barrels 124
Butter Churns 126

Cooling Beer	129
Special Barrels	130

Chapter 7 – Shelburne Barrel Factory — 135

Products Produced	135
Raising the Barrel	139
Making Barrelheads and Bottoms	142
Installing the Heads and Bottoms	144
Testing for leaks	145
Marking	146
Reproduction Barrels	146

Chapter 8 – Brooks Barrel Company — 149

Establishing the Barrel Company	149
Adjusting to Supplier Problems	150
Changing business Patterns	152
Ken Knox Joins Brooks Barrel	154
Knox Buys the Business	155
The Company Today	157

Chapter 9 – Barrels: Integrated into Our Culture — 159

Advertising	160
Port Scenes	162
The BIBLE, Bard, and the Barrel	164
Barrel Idioms	165
Barrel Nouns and Adjectives	168
Barrel Quotations	173
The Cracker Barrel	175
Song Lyrics that Mention Barrels	176
Aged in Barrels Today	177
State Seals	178
Barrel Legend and Lore	178
On a Less Serious Note	180
The Final Words	183

Glossary 185

Appendix A – Products in Barrels and Kegs 193

Appendix B – Barrel Gauging 195

Index 199

Acknowledgements

When attempting to research a subject such as the barrel, which is seldom found in any index, the help of a resource professional is seriously needed. I was fortunate to have the acquaintance of Edie White, a librarian at the Bel Air branch of the Harford County Public Library, who pointed me in a fruitful direction on numerous occasions. Her help is most appreciated.

Joseph Eagan and his staff in the periodicals department of the Enoch Pratt Free Library in Baltimore delivered to me bound copies of old magazines, which significantly benefited this effort. In particular a number outstanding illustrations from old issues of *Scientific American* are found in Chapter 6.

In Chapter 2 a special thanks goes to E. J. Raimondi for describing to me the engineering concept of "damage tolerance" that aided in explaining the barrel's robustness. The prior work of researchers Raymond Townsend of the Colonial Williamsburg Foundation; and Franklin E. Coyne, author of *The Development of the Cooperage Industry in the United States*, provided a rich source of background information for Chapter 3. Coyne's work and Kenneth Kilby's book on cooperage are much-cited references throughout.

"Making an American Barrel," Chapter 4, was significantly enhanced by the comments of Marshall Scheetz, apprentice cooper of the Colonial Williamsburg Foundation. In addition, friend and super draftsman, Bill Sisson, provided many of the illustrations.

Raymond and Donna Rhuland were most gracious in providing information about their Shelburne Barrel Factory discussed in Chapter 7. Likewise, retired Paul Brooks and current owner Ken Knox were gracious with their time when discussing the history of the Brooks Barrel Company presented in Chapter 8. Terry Stone, Erwin Anselm, and Jim Taylor of Cracker Barrel Old Country Store made individual contributions to Chapter 9. Arch Handy supplied the stamp of the post office and country store found on the back cover.

Erika Compton did great job of copyediting, making the draft much more readable. Her efforts are sincerely appreciated. My wife, Signe, provided encouragement and moral support throughout the writing effort, for which I am very grateful.

Jack L. Shagena, Jr. developed an interest in history at an early age while accompanying his parents on visits to Colonial Williamsburg. After graduating from Virginia Polytechnic Institute in 1959, he worked as an engineer, program manager, and aerospace executive for Bendix/AlliedSignal for thirty-four years. Upon retiring in 1993, he began researching Colonial and federal history and wrote *Brief History & Walking Tour of Historic Chesapeake City,* a former lock town along the nineteenth-century Chesapeake and Delaware Canal.

When researching and writing the script for an audiotape, *Historic Driving Tour of Cecil County*, a chance discovery of a Maryland roadside historic marker identified someone other than Robert Fulton as the inventor of the steamboat. His interest in history and engineering background coalesced and his book, *Who Really Invented the Steamboat? Fulton's* Clermont *Coup,* was published by Prometheus in June 2004.

Mr. Shagena, a retired registered professional engineer, has also written, *Jerusalem – A Restored Mill Village*, about a preserved community in Harford County, Maryland adjacent to Little Gunpowder Falls; *Bel Air Roller Mills: The Town's First Industry* that chronicles the contributions of Henry Reckord and sons to the industrial development of the Town of Bel Air; and *Humorous Recollections from Bendix Radio.*

He and his wife, Signe, have ten grandchildren and live in Harford County near Bel Air.

Chapter 1
Early History of the Wooden Container

Unlike clay pots or pottery chards, wooden containers, except in rare instances, have not survived over several millenniums, making it very difficult to know, with any certainty, how they may have been made. Any early history must rely on the limited writings of a few individuals and scant archeological data, or be approached tangentially to arrive at a plausible developmental timeline.

One thing, however, is clear: To produce a container the complexity of the cask or barrel required a set of tools. About these implements, Henry Ward Beecher has said, "A tool is but an extension of a man's hand, and a machine a complex tool. And he that invents a machine augments the power of a man and the well being of mankind." It will become obvious how tools in the hands of hard-working coopers made the containers of bulk commerce for thousands of years; but inevitably, with increased demand during the mid-nineteenth century, barrel-making machinery slowly replaced these skilled artisans.

Fundamental to effective woodworking tools was metal technology, so by briefly examining the slow but steady progress of metals in the copper, bronze, and iron ages, it should be possible to better understand how the barrel evolved. It is likely, however, some type of wooden tubs could have been made with earlier stone-age tools, as has been suggested by cooper and researcher Kenneth Kilby.[1]

When the first permanent English settlers arrived in Jamestown in 1607 they found the Native Americans in the area making log canoes by employing a controlled-burning technique. By this time the natives had discovered copper, and beads of it along with pearls were used for ornamentation, but not for tools. It is likely, therefore, the Stone Age man in other parts of the world had also employed the use of fanned fire with primitive flint or shell scrapers

HISTORY OF THE BARREL IN AMERICA

to remove the unwanted part of a section of a tree to produce a boat or primitive container (see figures 1-1 and 1-2).

Figure 1-1. Native Americans making a log canoe using fire. From Thomas Harriot, *A Briefe and True Report on the New Found Land of Virginia* (1590; reprint, New York: Dover Publications, 1972), p. 55.

The center portion of a short section of a large tree could be removed by placing hot coals on the end surface, fanning to promote burning, and dribbling water around the edges to keep the flame from progressing through the sides. By scraping out the charred remains, this would eventually produce a tub or perhaps a shallow bowl. There was always the likelihood that upon drying over time the sides of a tub would crack, so placing split saplings or strips of white oak, such as the ones used for baskets, around the outside helped maintain the container's integrity.

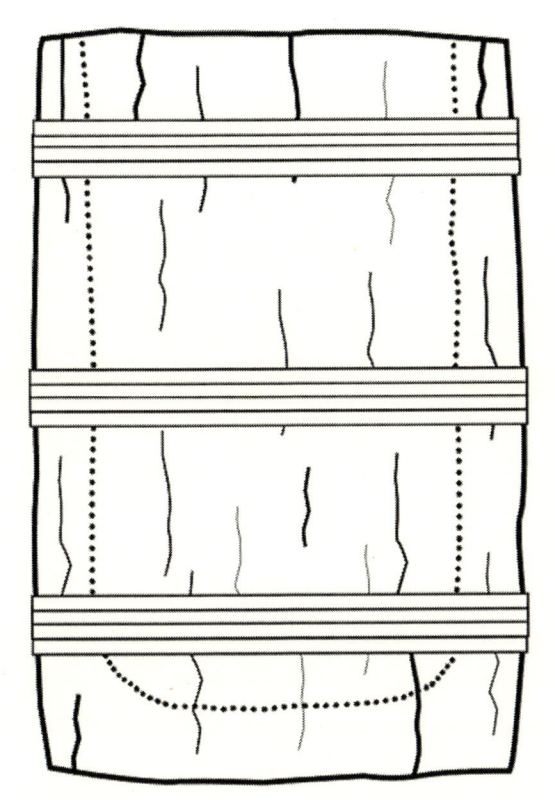

EARLY HISTORY OF THE WOODEN CONTAINER

Figure 1-2. Wooden tub hogged out of a tree trunk and kept from splitting apart by encircling with tightly-bound split sapings. Illustration by the author, 2004.

It was not until the metal ages, however, that wood could be cut and trimmed with sufficient accuracy to produce something similar to a cask. The illustration in figure 1-3 shows the relative times of the copper, bronze, and the start of the iron and steel ages. Also included chronologically are several important developments of the wooden container, which can be verified by archeological evidence and historical writings. The figure must be examined in concert with characteristics of the different metals to understand ability of each element or alloy to shape wood (see table 1-1).

HISTORY OF THE BARREL IN AMERICA

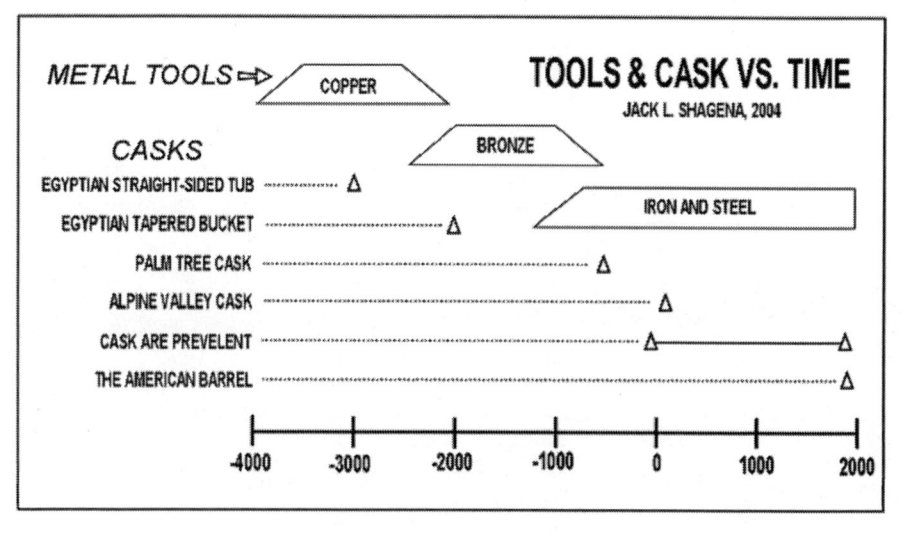

Figure 1-3. Shown is the development of metal tools and casks over time from 4000 BC to 2000 AD. Illustration by the author, 2004.[2]

Table 1-1. Comparison of the melting points and hardness of copper, bronze, iron, and steel.[3]

	Melting Point Degrees F	Hardness Brinell No.
Copper, hard 99.92% pure	1981	100
Bronze, hard 90% copper 10% tin	1830	200
Iron (carbon steel) 0.5% carbon	2802	240
Steel SAE 4340 Drawn 400 F	–	580

EARLY HISTORY OF THE WOODEN CONTAINER

Egyptian Straight-sided Tub

It has been reported by Kilby that a wall painting found in the tomb of Hesy-re, dating to about 2690 BC, showed a tub with straight-sided wooden slats held together by wooden hoops (see figure 1-4).[4] From the preceding figure 1-3, it is likely the container was made with copper tools, as it was about a half-millennium later (2500 BC) before bronze was generally introduced. The dates can only be approximated as other researchers note that, "there was a true Copper Age in Egypt up to about 2000 B.C., that is to say, a period during which pure copper was utilized . . ."[5]

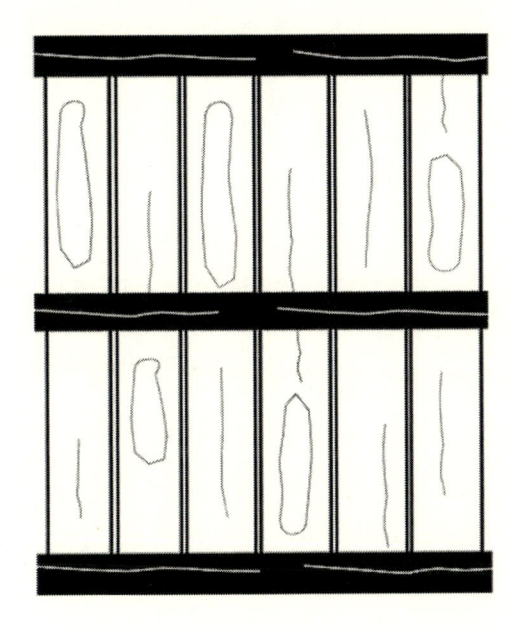

Figure 1-4. Early Egyptian wooden tub with staves and hoops. Illustration by the author, adapted from Kenneth Kilby, page 90.

From table 1-1 it can be noted that pure copper has a hardness of 100 when measured on the Brinell scale. In its natural state, or when smelted from ore, it solidifies to a much softer number of 45, and it is only through work-hardening that it can achieve an edge approximating the ability of cutting soft wood. After melting the metal at about 2,000 degrees Fahrenheit, knives could be made by pouring the liquid copper into clay molds with the approximate the shape of the object. The blade would be hammered to the desired thickness and the edge sharpened, also by hammering. At some point,

HISTORY OF THE BARREL IN AMERICA

the metal would begin to crack, so before that happened, the knife was annealed, that is, heated to below its melting point and allowed to slowly cool to the ambient temperature.

With such a knife, saw, and chisel, perhaps augmented with sharper flint tools, some woodworking on soft species would have been possible, but precision work would have been difficult. Probably the straight-sided tub shown in figure 1-4 was produced with copper tools.[6]

Egyptian Tapered Tub

It is possible that copper tools may have been considerably harder because of unavoidable amounts of other elements that invariably crept into the refining of copper ore. One of those metals was tin, and it was learned that the addition of ten percent of tin to copper would significantly improve the hardness, raising it to a value of 200, more than twice the pure metal. This new alloy was called bronze and today is known as phosphor bronze, a misnomer, but a name that persists. Bronze tools were not necessarily sharper than flint, but were more durable and could be made in any shape, such as a saw, file, chisel, saw, or knife, to do specialized jobs.

A painting showing tapered tubs filled with fresh or dried grapes, dating from about 1900 BC, was found on the wall of the Egyptian tomb of Beni Hasan.[7] It is likely the development of bronze tools facilitated the making of the curved and beveled edge staves which made up the side of the barrel. The bronze chisels made it easier to cut the groove into one end of each stave so the tub bottom could be held into place (see figure 1-5).

Figure 1-5. Painting of tapered tubs found in the tomb of Beni Hasan. From F. L. Griffith, ed., *Beni Hasan*, part I (London: Gilbert and Rivington, 1893), Tomb No. 2, Plate X.

EARLY HISTORY OF THE WOODEN CONTAINER

Use of a tapered design was a major step forward as it allowed the hoop to be pressed upward to tighten the staves one against the other.

Palm Tree Cask

What appears to be the first real evidence about the cask or barrel is found in the writings of Herodotus about the fifth century BC. He reported:

> The boats which come down the river to Babylon [the River Euphrates] are circular and made of skins. The frames which are of willow are cut in the country of the Armenians above Assyria, and on these which serve for hulls, a covering of skins is stretched outside, and thus the boats are made, without stem or stern, quite round like a shield. They are entirely filled with straw, and their cargo is put on board, after which they are suffered to float down the stream. Their chief freight is wine stored in casks made of the wood of the palm-tree. They are managed by two men who stand upright in them, each plying an oar, one pulling and the other pushing. The boats are of various sizes, some larger, some smaller; the biggest they reach as high as five thousand talents burthen. Each vessel has a live ass on board; those of larger size have more than one. When they reach Babylon, the cargo is landed and offered for sale; after which the men break up their boats, sell the straw and frames, and loading their asses with the skins, set off on their way back to Armenia. The current is too strong to allow a boat to go upstream, for which reason they make their boats of skins rather than wood. On their return they build fresh boats for the next voyage.[8]

About this quotation, Edward Hyams in his book *Dionysus: A Social History of the Wine Vine* goes on to note. "[I]t would seem that the Armenians were the first coopers, or they may have bought their wine-casks in Assyria."[9] Since wood rarely leaves traces for the archeologist, this is difficult to know for certain.

Alpine Valley Cask

Pliny the elder (23-79 BC), writing a half millennium later, ascribes the invention of the wooden cask to the inhabitants of the Alpine Valley.[10] By this time, iron and steel tools had become available, so making a container from a harder wood such as oak would have become more practical. Note in table 1-1 that iron with a

HISTORY OF THE BARREL IN AMERICA

carbon content of 0.5 percent produced a harder metal than bronze and by additional working in a fossil-fueled furnace, more carbon would have been imparted, yielding even harder steel. Today SAE 4340 steel has a hardness of 580 but it is doubtful the early metalworkers would have approached such a value through trial and error. Nevertheless, introduction of iron and steel opened new possibilities in accurately shaping hard woods and later in shaping metal for machines.

As to Pliny's claim that the cask came from the Celts in the Alpine Valley, it appears he was not aware of the writing by Herodotus, and this may have been his first exposure to the wooden containers.

Casks Are Prevalent and The American Barrel

Kilby concluded that by the first century BC, "barrels were being used for wine, beer, milk, butter and water, and buckets and tubs must have been commonplace."[11] As the barrel was becoming the container of choice for shipping bulk goods, it would quickly spread to all parts of the trading world and be copied if not already previously developed. Across the globe it would enjoy a long life of 2,000 years (see figures 1-6, 1-7, and 1-8).

Figure 1-6. Costumes of the day from the Queen Anne period (1702-14) showing a worker carrying a barrel. From James Hunter, *The Golden Treasury*, vol. 1 (Philadelphia: Illustrated Publishing, 1888), page 107

EARLY HISTORY OF THE WOODEN CONTAINER

Figure 1-7. Dutch coopers making a barrel in 1568. From Das Ständebuch, drawn by Jost Amman and from Graham Blackburn, *Woodworking Handtools, Instruments and Devices* (New York: Simon and Schuster, 1974), page 86.

HISTORY OF THE BARREL IN AMERICA

Figure 1-8. Barrel making taken from *Diderot and D'Alembert*, Encyclopédie (1751-65) as found in Louis B. Wright, *Everyday Life in Colonial America* (New York: G. P. Putnam's Sons, 1905), page 93.

In America, the barrel would reign supreme for more than three hundreds years. Eventually, steel and plastic containers would replace the wooden barrel, but even then, it would be retained in the niche markets of wine, distilled spirits, and seasonings.

Was the Barrel Invented?

Although it has been suggested the barrel is an invention,[12] it is most probable the container was incrementally developed over a long period by a series of improvements known as innovations. An innovation may be thought of as *improving* the way something is done, for example, curving the blade of a kitchen knife so it "rocked" up an down on a cutting board while sliding a carrot or celery under the blade to produced chopped vegetables. An invention, however, would *change* the way something is done such as substituting a food processor for the knife and cutting board.[13]

It has been noted that straight-sided wooden buckets, held together with hoops made of strips of wood, have been observed on

EARLY HISTORY OF THE WOODEN CONTAINER

Egyptian paintings dating to 2690 BC. So it's likely the straight-sided bucket evolved to one with tapered sides where it then became possible to drive on a hoop and force the staves together. At about the same time, the V-groove was perfected. It provided seating for the container's bottom when trimmed in a complementary manner. These two innovations produced a decided improvement in the bucket's practical utility, as the staves were in compression, the hoops in tension and the device, and if carefully crafted, could be watertight.

Making a straight-sided bucket watertight meant the hoops had to force the staves tightly together. With the later-evolved tapered design, this could be accomplished by driving the hoops to the larger diameter of the container, but with parallel staves no such advantage accrued. So was it possible to get the hoop in tension and the staves in compression?

One approach would have been to use thoroughly dried wood for the staves and bottom, and green strips of wood for the hoops. In America, hoops were made from wood with high longitudinal strength, such as oak, elm, or hickory. White oak, in particular, when green, can be pulled into thin strips, which were also used for basket weaving.

Such unseasoned or green strips of wood will be slightly shorter when allowed to dry out, but the difference is only 0.1 to 0.3 percent and can be ignored. Radially across the grain, however, the amount of increase of dry white oak when fully swollen is 9 percent.[14]

If a straight-sided bucket is made with hoops of green wood, but seasoned staves and a seasoned bottom, it should be possible to assemble the pieces fairly tightly together, then immerse the container in water. The staves and bottom will swell, and confined by the hoops, will press the joints snugly together to make the container watertight. Such an arrangement could suffice for a well bucket confined to a wet environment, but would probably not work as a transportation container in a dry environment.

There was, however, at least one competing technology for containers, namely clay vessels called amphorae, used by the Greeks and early Romans. These were used to transport high-value liquids such as oil and wine, but were rather fragile. Archeologists have found shards of amphorae dating up to the second century AD, but they become scarce thereafter.[15] This provides circumstantial evidence that they were replaced with another technology believed to be the barrel. This evidence seems to roughly correlate with Pliny's observation of wooden casks from Cisalpine Gaul transporting wine, as it appears to coincide with the gradual replacement of amphorae as the transportation vessel of choice. Evidence, though, is rather sketchy and far from conclusive.

The transition from a straight-sided container, to a tapered bucket, to a barrel would have likely occurred over a long period of time as skilled artisans made incremental improvements or so-called innovations. Following this supposition, the author advances a hypothesis for this technological transition that culminated in the barrel. It will be left to future archeologists and other researchers to either confirm or debunk the hypothesis, but in any case, this postulated technical evolution might provide a modicum of insight for other investigators.

Once it was routinely possible to produce a tight seal between individual staves, and the staves and the bottom of the bucket, it would have logically occurred to someone that a top was needed to make it a sealed container. A fill hole may have been placed in a stave, but more likely was in the top located on the side adjacent to the staves. This construction would have been fairly rugged, but would lack a key element intrinsic in the barrel of being its own wheel at a time when motive power was supplied by human or animal muscle. This is further discussed in Chapter 2.

There also existed a subtle structural problem with the longevity of the tapered design. The staves could be held tight against the top and bottom by simply driving the hoops to a wider portion of the structure. But what if a leak occurred through a gap in the staves somewhere between the top and bottom hoops? Applying a middle hoop would force the staves back together, but would tend to loosen the hoop at the top and bottom as well as slightly unseat the top and bottom heads in the V-groove possible precipitating a leak. A more immediate practical solution for someone transporting the container would be to drive thin strips of wood between the leaking staves. This would cause the adjacent staves to slightly bow outward, possibly disrupting the seal between the stave and heads, but the hoops at the

EARLY HISTORY OF THE WOODEN CONTAINER

top and bottom in this case would actually be tightened, hence a better solution (see figures 1-9 and 1-10).

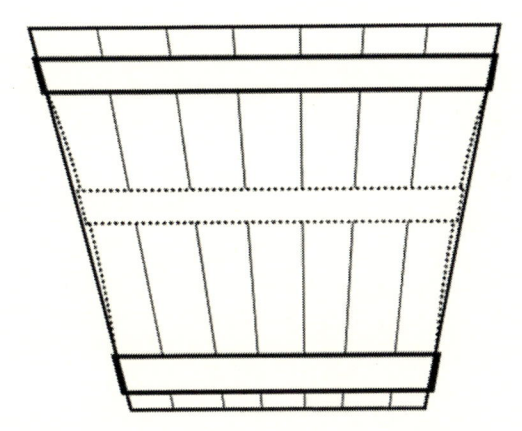

Figure 1-9. Bucket with a head on both the top and bottom making it a closed container filled through a bunghole. If a leak developed between the staves, it could be corrected by the application of the middle hoop shown dotted, but this compresses the center possibly loosening the top and bottom hoops. A better solution is to drive thin wedges between the offending staves. Illustration by the author, 2004.

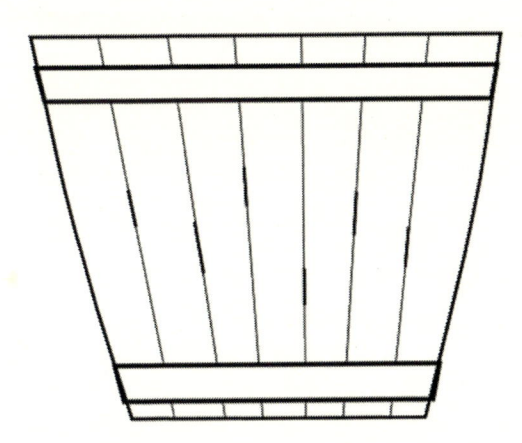

Figure 1-10. The same container shown in figure 1-9, but here wedges of wood have been inserted between the staves to stop leaks. Depending on the number of repairs (exaggerated here), this causes the container to develop a slight, however, almost imperceptible bulge, which to an observant cooper would be the clue to the development of a barrel. Illustration by the author, 2004.

Interestingly, the slightly bulging staves would have provided a serendipitous clue to the astute artesian who repaired the cask. Why not deliberately make the staves a slight bit wider in the middle (as the wooden shims had effectively done) thereby causing the staves to slightly bow in the middle as the container was constructed? Once this principle was recognized, it was only a short leap to make double-tapered staves much longer and the barrel was born (see figure 1-11).

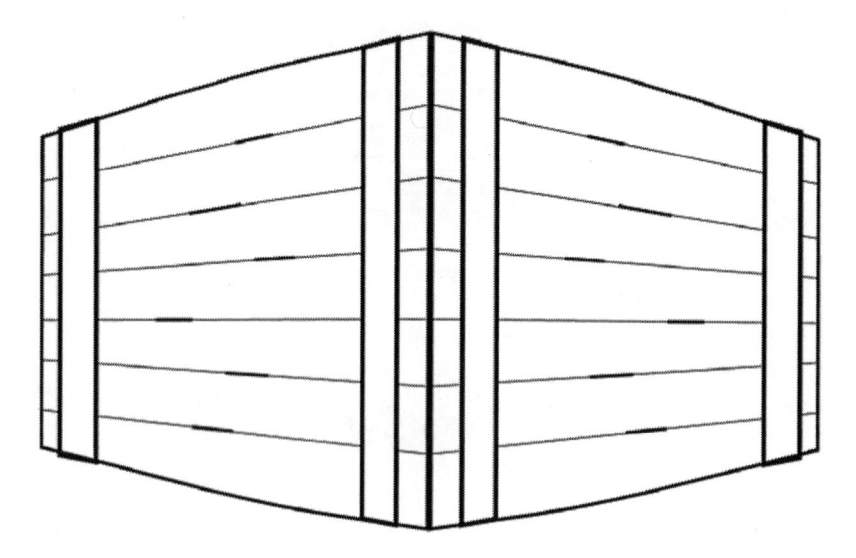

Figure 1-11. Intellectually imagining two closed buckets placed end-to-end would have provided a clue that such an integrated structure would provide significant advantages as a container for liquids. Illustration by the author, 2004.

If there had been an intellectual leap from the straight-sided sealed bucket to a barrel, no doubt this would qualify as an invention, as it changed, not improved, the way the container was made. This is a necessary component of invention, as we know it today, but at the time such a concept could have been recognized intellectually but was not codified into any laws that provided the inventor any special privileges.

The genius of the barrel is the use of staves tapered at each end, *bent* and held in place by hoops. It now becomes possible to drive a hoop tighter to increase the pressure between staves; hence,

EARLY HISTORY OF THE WOODEN CONTAINER

mitigating or stopping a leak without adversely impacting the seal between the heads and staves. The bulging middle produces a rounded surface known as the bilge or pitch that allows the container to be safely rotated and rolled without damaging its structural integrity. So perfect was the historical design, it has undergone almost no change from its inception to today.

HISTORY OF THE BARREL IN AMERICA

[1] Kenneth Kilby, *The Cooper and His Trade* (1977; reprint, Fresno, CA: Linden Publishing, 1977), p. 88.
[2] Glyn Daniel, ed., *The Illustrated Encyclopedia of Archaeology* (New York: Thomas Y. Crowell, 1877). This was the primary source for determining the approximate dates for the use of metal tools.
[3] Theodore Braumeister, ed., *Mechanical Engineers' Handbook* (New York: McGraw-Hill, 1958). Information from pp. 5-5, 6-59, 6-80, 6-81.
[4] Kilby, *The Cooper and His Trade*, p. 91.
[5] T. K. Derry and Trevor I. Williams, *A Short History of Technology: From the Earliest Times to A.D. 1900* (New York: Dover, 1960), p. 117.
[6] In the period 2494-2435 BC, Egyptian files were made by punching holes in a copper sheet and attaching to a stick. See Jonathan Fairbanks, "Craft Processes and Images: Visual Sources for the Study of the Craftsman," Ian M. G. Quimby, ed., *The Craftsman in Early America* (New York: W.W. Norton & Co., 1984), p. 311.
[7] Kilby, *The Cooper and His Trade*, p. 91
[8] As quoted in Edward Hyams, *Dionysus: A Social History of the Wine Vine* (New York: MacMillan, 1965), p. 40.
[9] Ibid, p. 49.
[10] *The Encyclopedia Britannica, A Dictionary of Arts, Sciences and General Literature*, 25 vols. (Chicago: Warner, 1894) 6:338.
[11] Kilby, *The Cooper and His Trade*, p. 95.
[12] Ibid., p. 3. William B. Sprague, "The Cooper," *The Chronicle of the Early American Industries Association*, June 1938, 2:33.
[13] For a discussion of innovation versus invention, see Jack L. Shagena, *Who Really Invented the Steamboat? : Fulton's Clermont Coup* (Amherst, NY: Humanity, 2004), pp. 39–65.
[14] Baumeister, ed., *Mechanical Engineers' Handbook*, p. 6-147.
[15] K. Kilby, *The Village Cooper* (Great Britain: CIT Printing, 1998), p.5.

Chapter 2

The Robust Barrel: Handle with Care?

Description of the Barrel

The barrel is a thin-walled cylinder with a bulging middle made of longitudinally-tapered wooden slats of varying widths, called staves, each having slightly beveled edges that fit closely together and held in compression by strong outside hoops. Hoops were formerly made of strips of wood, but now of metal, usually iron, with the ends riveted together or sometimes with a loop of wire twisted on the ends. Circular wooden discs with tapered edges, called heads, generally made of several pieces of wood dowelled together on the edges, are placed in parallel planes inside U- or V-grooves near the ends of the bent staves and compressed in place with a hoop around the outside.

It is truly remarkable a container was developed and remained substantively unchanged for hundreds of years. Its robustness stems from the barrel's unique structure that provides substance to its durability and longevity. Of the design, it has been noted in a cooperage catalog:

> Through the centuries the wooden barrel is the only container that has withstood the genius of man to improve upon the amazing principle on which it is built. As each stave rests in position with its neighbor, and all are bound together by hoop pressure from the outside, the "double-arch" principle of STRENGTH is formed.[1]

Another barrel expert and author of *The Development of the Cooperage Industry in the United States,* Franklin Coyne has observed:

> [The barrel] without doubt [is] the strongest possible container for any product, it makes one marvel at its simplicity and perfection, and any real improvement in its construction would be almost an impossibility.

> [W]hile the manufacturer of tight barrels is a very ancient trade there has been very little, if any, real improvement made in the details of construction, which considered as a whole, is in reality a work of art...[2]

Over the years the barrel has "been taken for granted" as its contents, not the container itself, was valued. If, as Coyne suggests it is a "work of art," perhaps a serious examination of the barrel's uniqueness may provide insights to future package engineers who will be designing other containers.

Robustness Examined

Mechanical devices, which over time deliver satisfactory performance despite occasional unintended minor damage, develop a reputation for being rugged or robust. The damage is usually not premeditated, occurring as a result of normal use for which the device was intended. Sometimes robustness can be achieved by deliberate over-design, such as making something stronger, invariably heaver, and more cumbersome than actually required. Over time, however, such devices will yield to new designs that exhibit better use to the user.

One example of robustness is found in the flashlight, which may be dropped or bumped, but continues to provide a bright steady beam. Another, of course, is the sturdy barrel, which has survived for more than two millenniums virtually unchanged, lending credence to its robustness.

In the 1960s, engineers at Wright Paterson Air Force Base in Dayton, Ohio, began to study miniscule cracks in aircraft structures with the intention of developing a model to predict at what point such minor damage required corrective action to maintain aircraft safety. This led to the concept of "damage tolerance," that is, the ability of an assembly or individual component to continue to function satisfactorily despite minor damage that is the direct result of use.[3] Applied to the barrel, the damage tolerance concept has a parallel as discussed below.

THE ROBUST BARREL: HANDLE WITH CARE?

The Pre-Stressed Barrel

Today, this type of construction is identified as "pre-stressed," a design technique that takes advantage of intrinsically desirable characteristics found in different materials. Probably the most familiar example is using the tensile strength of steel combined with the compressive strength and heat resistance of concrete to make structural beams for building construction. As can be seen in figure 2-1, the protruding ends of the steel bars are placed in tension, and concrete, contained by a form, is poured around. After the concrete has hardened, the tension is released, which causes the concrete to be compressed.

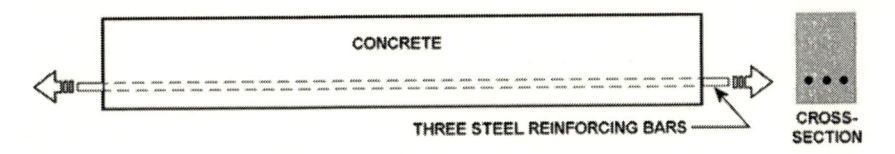

Figure 2-1. A pre-stressed beam made of steel reinforcing bars and concrete. Such an arrangement yields a beam with good structural characteristics. The concrete adheres to the surface-deformed round bars located close to the bottom where tension is concentrated when the beam is loaded. Illustration by the author, 2004.

The pre-stressed beam above has a parallel with the barrel shown in figure 2-2. The edges of the staves are held in compression by the metal hoops in tension. This configuration forces each stave tightly against its neighbor, as well as tightly against the heads of the container confined in a V-groove. For a barrel that contains fresh water for example, the weight of the liquid actually creates a pressure that tends to force the staves apart, which can produce a leak. For a barrel three feet high resting on one end, the pressure will be 187 pounds per square foot on the bottom head. The staves at the bottom also must withstand the same pressure that decreases to zero at the top of the stave level with the water's surface. It is only the hoops driven tightly down toward the bulge that keep the staves in compression that opposes the internal pressure, and therefore keeps the barrel tight and free from leaks.

HISTORY OF THE BARREL IN AMERICA

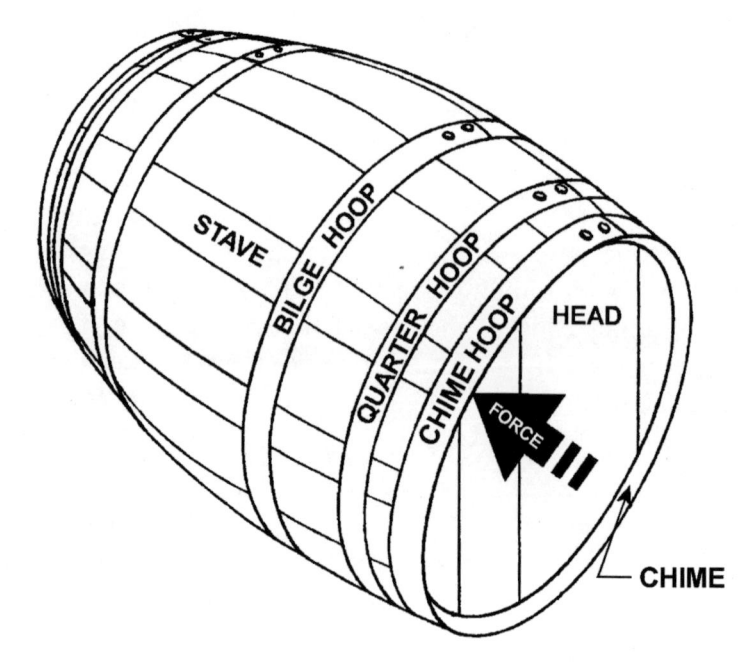

Figure 2-2. A barrel with the parts labeled and with an end force applied to one of the stave. Illustration by the author, 2004.

This pre-stressed arrangement is the real secret of the barrel's water tightness, but there are additional generally unobserved important aspects of the design. The barrel depicted in figure 2-2 is being subjected to an external force, shown by the arrow. The force is pressing against a single stave and not the barrel's chime hoop.

As the stave is tapered on each end and wider in the center, the three hoops on the far end would have to expand to accompany any movement. As the hoops are in tension, having been driven onto the staves forcing them tightly together, this cannot easily happen. Therefore, the single stave is integrated into the whole container in such a way to provide a unified structural integrity found in only the best mechanical designs.

There is more to this particular aspect of the barrel design that can be seen in the cross-sectional view shown in figure 2-3. The same previously applied force is shown, but also observe the barrelheads, fitted into the V-groove, also constrict the movement of a stave.

THE ROBUST BARREL: HANDLE WITH CARE?

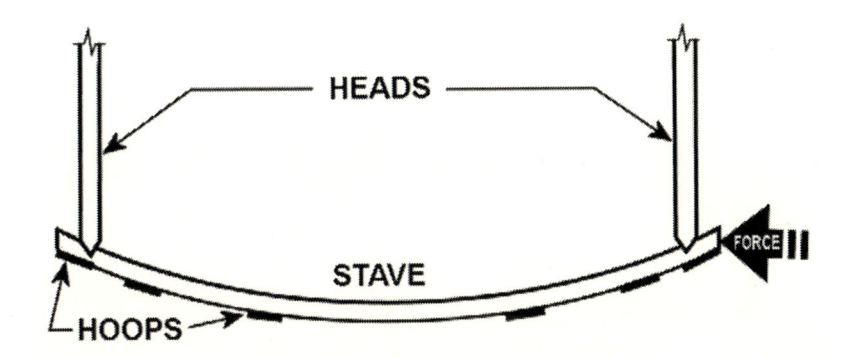

Figure 2-3. Cross-section of a portion of a barrel is depicted showing how an applied force is restrained by the barrelhead, which locks the stave in place with the V-groove. Illustration by the author, 2004.

In terms of damage tolerance, consider the barrel being dropped a few inches onto one edge of the chime, producing a force as shown in figure 2-3, but in this case applied simultaneously to both the stave and the chime hoop. The stave is relatively fragile as a couple of inches away is the croze or V-groove, making it susceptible to breaking across this line. The primary protection making it tolerant to withstand this damage is the chime hoop, which absorbs some of the impact by distributing it around the entire end of the barrel's circumference. Hence, the design is damage tolerant, no doubt a characteristic that evolved over a period of time.

A force applied to the side of a barrel stave, not the hoop, is shown below in figure 2-4. In this case, stave B is depicted slightly displaced, and because of the taper on its edges, causes the staves on either side A and C to slightly move (note arrows), increasing the tension on the hoop. Thus it can be observed the application of a force to one stave causes the force to be distributed throughout the entire structure making the barrel quite robust.

Again, another example of damage tolerance can be observed if a transient impact initially forces stave B inward, but upon recoiling there can momentarily exist a slight separation from adjacent staves A and C, allowing a small amount of liquid to escape. The fundamental integrity of the container, however, is not impacted unless the stave is cracked or otherwise damaged.

HISTORY OF THE BARREL IN AMERICA

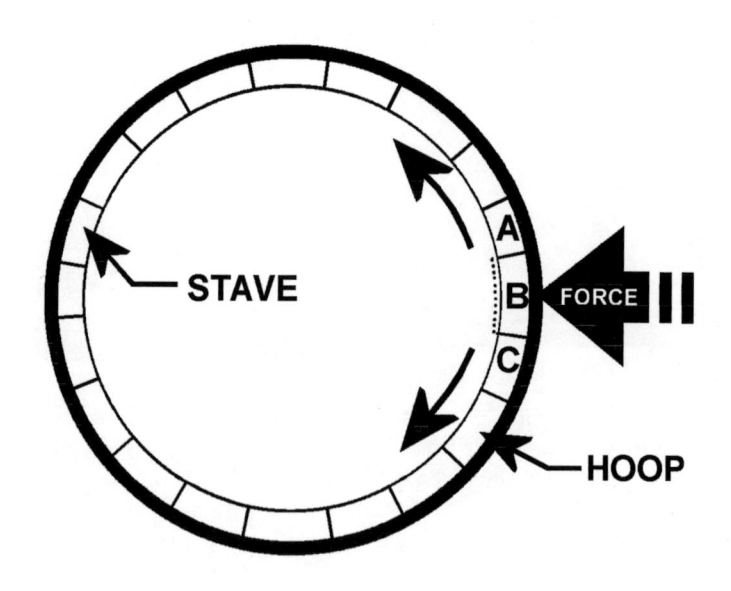

Figure 2-4. Cross-section of a barrel with an external force applied to the side of one of the staves. Illustration by the author, 2004.

Repeated occurrences of such an action would have adverse consequences if one stave were much harder the other. It is possible cooper Kenneth Kilby was intuitively aware of the problem when he wrote about raising a barrel: "The staves must be matched according to toughness. If a soft stave is placed between two hard ones it will be forced out outwards and crack either in the firing or later in wear."[4]

Another aspect of fault-tolerant design leading to robustness can be understood by referring back to figure 2-2. Suppose the force is shown pressing against one of the pieces of the head instead of a stave. As each piece in the head is dowelled to its neighbor, the force is distributed throughout the entire head again, achieving a more robust design.

The Wheel Comparison

Although not as old as the barrel, the wooden-spoked wheel with a metal tire also is a pre-stressed structure and provides an interesting comparison. It is shown in figure 2-5.

THE ROBUST BARREL: HANDLE WITH CARE?

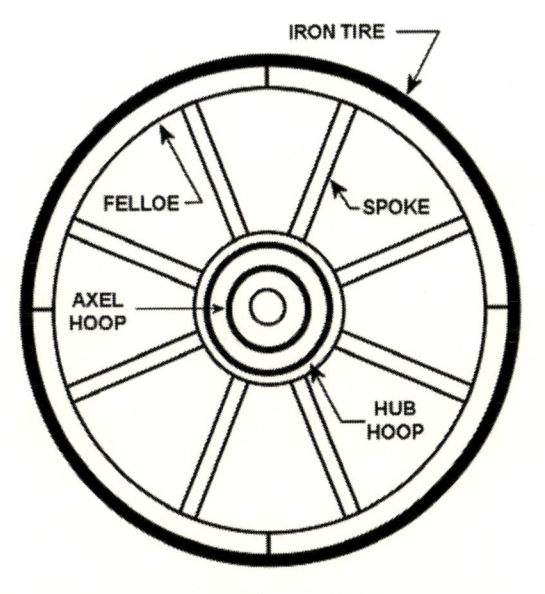

Figure 2-5. The wheel, like the barrel, is a pre-stressed structure, which is held in compression by the iron tire. Illustration by the author, 2004.

The iron tire is made slightly smaller than the diameter comprised by the four felloes that make up the outside of the wooden wheel. The tire is heated causing expansion, whereby it is slipped over the wheel and cooled with buckets of water. As the tire cools and contracts, it forces the felloes and spokes into the hub creating a pre-stressed entity. Additionally much smaller metal rings or hoops are driven over the hub, keeping the wood around the spokes and axel from splitting, see figure 2-6.

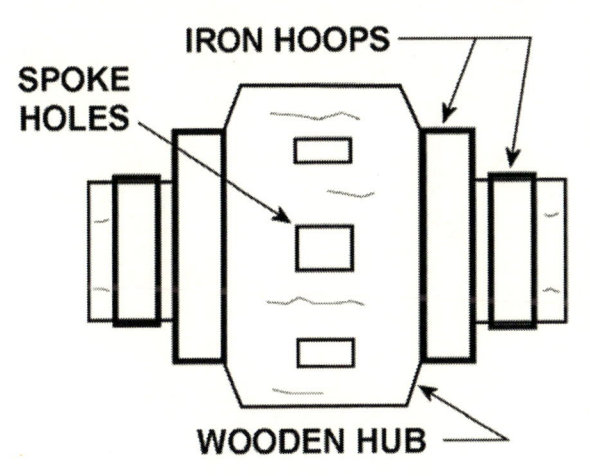

Figure 2-6. The hub of a wooden wheel usually made from elm, with iron hoops installed to keep the hub and the axel hole from splitting the wood. Illustration by the author, 2004.

HISTORY OF THE BARREL IN AMERICA

Speculation on the Barrel Shape

For years the egg has been revered as Mother Nature's perfect container. This prompted magazine writer Luis Marden, when describing cooperage at Colonial Williamsburg, to use an egg/barrel analogy noting, "In almost no other object made by man does form follow function so purely as in a barrel."[5]

Advertisements for packaging in the 1960s prominently featured the egg and likened it to new package designs. Could the egg have been the inspiration for a barrel? To examine this curiosity, a hole was poked in the side of an egg and drained the contents. A short rubber band was then stretched lengthwise around the egg dividing it into two halves. A pencil was used to draw a line alongside the rubber band, whence the eggshell was dissected along the line with sharp scissors. It was placed on a scanner and the image on the left of figure 2-7 was produced.

By equally truncating the top and bottom, the image on the right was created, which, perhaps not too surprisingly, has the recognizable shape of a barrel. A coincidence? Most likely, as it would have been a gigantic step to go from an egg to a barrel, and improvement in wooden containers evolved over a long period of time with the barrel eventually becoming the pinnacle of perfection.

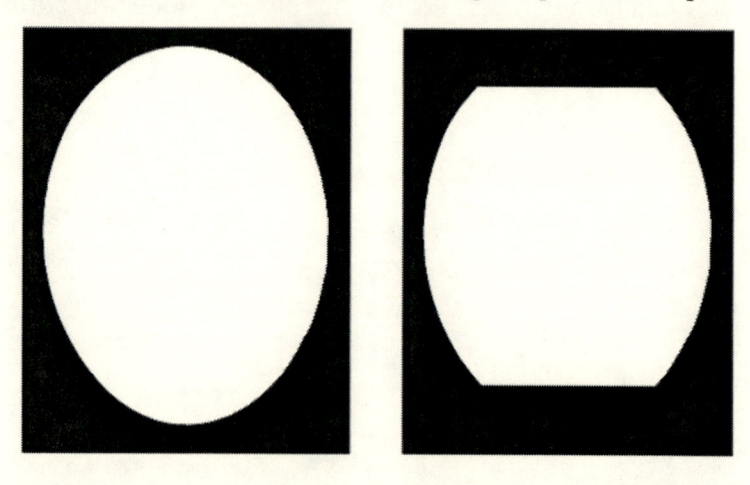

Figure 2-7. Left is the profile of a chicken egg. On the right is the same profile, but truncated on the top and bottom, producing a barrel-like image. Illustrations by the author, 2004.

THE ROBUST BARREL: HANDLE WITH CARE?

Over Niagara Falls

Annie Edson Taylor had for many years lived a vagabond life traveling around America as a dance teacher. At age sixty-three she found herself in Bay City, Michigan where she had contemplated her future of being very poor and no longer having her girlish figure or attractive looks she once enjoyed.

How to continue to dress properly and maintain appearances was very important, but dancing prospects had seriously dwindled so a new plan was desperately needed. It was 1901, the year of the Pan-American Exposition in Buffalo, and as she read the newspaper about the people flocking to see the exposition and going on to see the falls, she also noticed a story about Carlisle Graham. He was an obsessive cooper who was taking his fifth ride through the rapids and whirlpool below the falls.

Suddenly the idea of being the first person to go *over* Niagara Falls in a barrel struck her. The barrel was well known as being the sturdiest container available and Taylor may have been aware of a barrel like the one in Missouri that survived a tornado in 1891 (see figure 2-8).

Surely she thought going over the falls and surviving would bring her fame with the accompanying fortune, so this plucky senior, down on her luck, decided it was worth a try. She needed two things: a barrel, and an agent to promote the event. She got the West Bay Cooperage Company of Buffalo[6] to make the barrel and found Frank M. "Tussie" Russell of Bay City, who had experience as a carnival promoter. The promoter parted his slick-down hair in the middle, stood a tad higher than Taylor at about five feet, four inches, and at thirty-five was young enough to be her son. Thinking she would draw more sightseers to the falls (see figure 2-9) by being younger, she told him she was forty-two.

HISTORY OF THE BARREL IN AMERICA

Figure 2-8. On May 20, 1891 a tornado passed through Missouri near Centralia causing damage to many structures. The remains of a house and barn are shown above and most surprising is what appears to be a still intact barrel. From *Scientific American*, August 15, 1891.

On September 22, 1901, Russell announced in the Bay City *Times-Tribune* that an unnamed client was planning a trip over Niagara Falls in a barrel, but declined to provide information as to Taylor's identity or motivations. Several weeks later, on October 11, he arrived at Niagara Falls, New York, and announced to the press that Annie Taylor would make the plunge, stating, "She was a widow, forty-two years old, intelligent and adventuresome," and continued to ramble on hyping her risk-taking background.[7]

Taylor arrived on October 13 and met the press. One journalist described her as "agile, athletic and strong," but most were skeptical of her age, placing her closer to fifty.[8] As she prepared for her attempt, Russell found Fred Truesdale, an expert river man, who tested Taylor's barrel over the falls with a cat on October 18. The destiny of the feline, however, remains in dispute.

THE ROBUST BARREL: HANDLE WITH CARE?

Figure 2-9. Niagara Fall as seen in about 1863. From D. M. Warren, Common-School Geography: *An Elementary Treatise on Mathematical, Physical, and Political Geography* (Philadelphia: H. Cowerwait and Co., 1863), page 25.

Taylor said she was ready and a Sunday crowd gathered to watch, but she did not appear. Her promoter provided an excuse and the event was rescheduled for Wednesday, but bad weather forced a second postponement. One newspaper claimed in a headline it was all "A GIGANTIC HOAX!" By October 24, however Taylor was prepared to go, saying "au revoir" rather than goodbye. The head for the barrel, with her inside, was put in place, the container pumped full of air with a bicycle pump, and she was set afloat above the falls.

If the barrel survived the falls, it could get trapped for hours in the turbulence below, and it was believed the air pressure inside would allow her to breathe for a sustained period of time. What was not factored in, however, was the barrel was not airtight. A chink wide enough to allow light to pass through came to Taylor's attention. A rag was forced into the crack from the outside but the fabric failed to stop water from seeping in. It was too late, though, as she was on her way.

Strapped to the inside and cushioned with pillows, the barrel dubbed *Maid of the Mist* dropped over an initial forty-foot fall, remained intact, and headed toward the brink of the horseshoe. The barrel fell about one hundred sixty feet, achieving a speed of about seventy miles per hour as it splashed down. It shot up out of the water, plunged again, but quickly washed against the rocks near the side. The barrel was retrieved and a much battered and bruised Taylor was finally pulled out. She was badly shaken, but alive, and became the first person to accomplish the daring feat. The press recorded a few words she was able to utter, "If it was my dying breath, I would caution anyone against attempting the feat. I will never go over the Falls again. I would sooner walk up to the mouth of a cannon, knowing it was going to blow me to pieces than make another trip over the fall[s]."[9]

The wooden container, however, survived without damage and the November 1901 issue of *Barrel and Box* magazine recorded:

> The barrel was constructed especially for the purpose and we are pleased to note that it stood the racket and carried the lady safely over the fall with only a few bruises. The barrel was 4½ feet high and about 3 feet in diameter; and was fitted with leather harnesses, cushions, etc., on the inside, as protection from severe concussions. Mrs. Taylor went over the falls simply to gain notoriety so that she could better herself financially thereby, and while this is better than some ways in which some seek notoriety and while we are pleased with the ability of our coopers to make a barrel that will withstand the racket, still, the lady is old enough to have more gumption, and she ought to have been spanked and put to bed instead of taking such a foolish trip.[10]

Taylor had hoped for fame and fortune – she acquired a modicum of fame, but fortune eluded her. Part of the reason stemmed for her snobbish dislike of some public relation venues for money making, such as the motion picture industry, which had, in her mind, not yet achieved respectability. There were also disputes with her agent and for a while her famous barrel disappeared, was recovered, but vanished again. She ordered an exact replica and for many years sat outside on the sidewalk of the New England Restaurant in Niagara Falls selling and signing postcards and being photographed by tourists. She died in 1921 at age eighty-two; her feat eclipsed by the more flamboyant Bobbie Leach, who had gone over the falls in 1911 and also lived to tell the story.

THE ROBUST BARREL: HANDLE WITH CARE?

Figure 2-10. Annie Edson Taylor standing beside the barrel she rode over Niagara Fall and survived. From Charles Carlin Parish, *Queen of the Mist: The Story of Annie Edson Taylor* (Interlaken, NY: Heart of Lakes Publishing, 1987), cover.

Handle with Care?

The barrel, which can withstand the wrath of a tornado or fury of Niagara Falls, would seem to be virtually indestructible, so why should care be exercised in its handling? The Associated Cooperage Industries of America published an issue of *The Wooden Barrel Manual* about 1944, a portion of which addressed a few simple rules for handling the containers. It is likely the industry fully recognized the barrel enjoyed a reputation for being robust, but also knew the application of the guidelines would further enhance the barrel's reputation.

HISTORY OF THE BARREL IN AMERICA

Two ways identified as being acceptable and recommended in handling barrels are spinning and rolling on the bilge, the protruding belly of the barrel. These actions are shown in figure 2-11.

Figure 2-11. A barrel can safely be spun on its bilge to "head" it in the right direction, and then rolled on its bilge to move it to the desired location. Illustrations by the author, 2004.

Do not roll a barrel over a rough surface such as a cobblestone road or over railroad tracks, "As most tight barrels used to carry liquids are lined with an inner coating of glue, paraffin or silicate. These coatings are sufficiently resilient to withstand the shocks of ordinary handling, but rough treatment may cause the lining to break at the joints, causing the barrel to leak."[11] The chime, the edge of the staves extending beyond the head, has much less strength when compared with the bilge, so, "never roll a barrel on it edge."

Upending a barrel, that is righting a barrel that is lying on it bilge to standing on its end, can be done by grasping by the chime and rocking to an upright position. When moving barrels for one elevation to another, remember damage can be caused by shock such as dropping even a few inches, so always "ease" it down, and "ease" it to a stop.

There are a number of ways to hoist barrels for lowering into the hull of a ship. One of these ways is depicted in figure 2-12.

THE ROBUST BARREL: HANDLE WITH CARE?

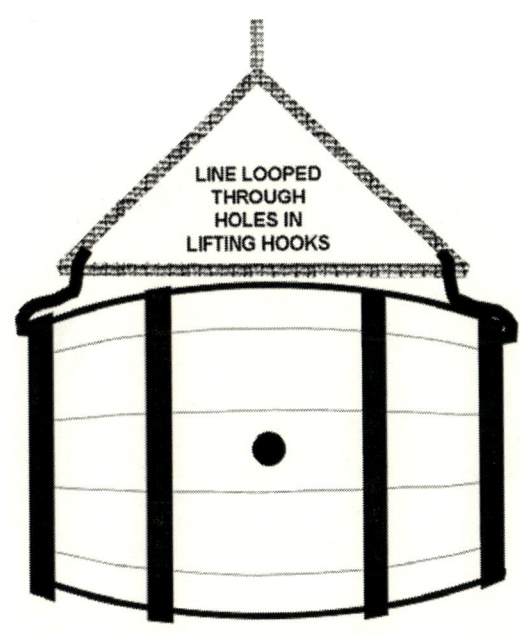

Figure 2-12. Barrels can be safely lifted through the use of two curved hooks that are placed under the chime and secured by a lifting line that holds the hooks in place. Illustration by the author, 2004.

In other cases, numerous rope configurations have been developed to encompass the barrel, while a net can also be used to hoist a number of barrels at the same time. A safe hoisting using only a line is shown in figure 2-13.

Figure 2-13. Two techniques for hoisting barrels. From *Scientific American,* August 21, 1880, page 115.

HISTORY OF THE BARREL IN AMERICA

Removing the Bung

While not immediately obvious, the bung (stopper) must be flush with the bunghole so when rolling the barrel on the bilge, no unnecessary stress will be transmitted to the bung stave. Obviously, this poses a problem when removing the bung, as there is not a surface above the stave to work a blade into and pry the bung out. A special lightweight spring-handled hammer called a bung-tapper solved the problem (see figure 2-14). The reason for the springiness of the handle is not immediately obvious, but will be covered in the following paragraphs.

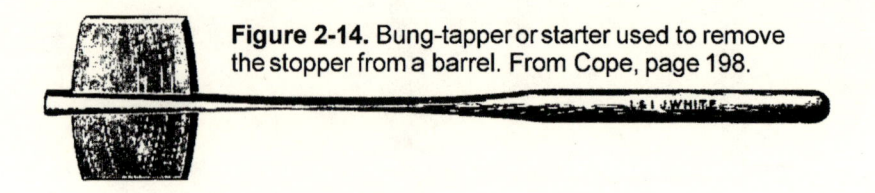

Figure 2-14. Bung-tapper or starter used to remove the stopper from a barrel. From Cope, page 198.

The bung-tapper is used to strike the bung stave in the immediately vicinity of the stopper, as shown by the locations marked "X" in figure 2-15. Referring back to figure 2-4, however, the reader will note that a force on a stave will cause it to be momentarily displaced an incremental amount, but being held in tension by the adjacent staves as a result of the hoops, the stave will immediately revert into its original position once the force is removed.

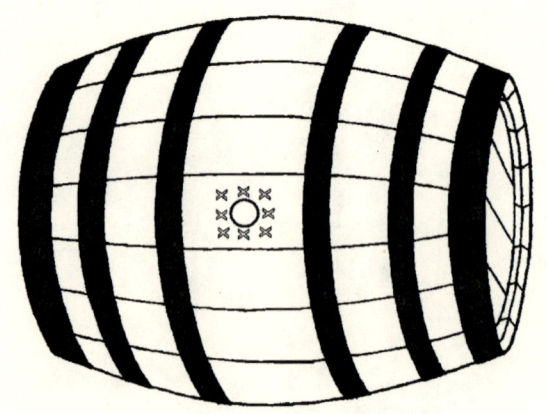

Figure 2-15. Top view of a barrel with the positions marked "X" indicating where the bung stave is tapped to remove the stopper. Illustration by the author, 2004.

THE ROBUST BARREL: HANDLE WITH CARE?

Observe that the bung or stopper is not struck, only the stave surrounding the stopper, but as the stave moves down the bung will try to follow being tightly seated in the bunghole. The bung, however, has some weight or mass, and not being acted on directly by a striking force, will "attempt" to remain in place. Repeated actions of the bung-tapper will gradually cause the stopper to rise above the bunghole where it can be easily removed.

So why does the bung-tapper have a spring handle? If an ordinary hammer were used, this would also force the bung out, but a spring handle makes the tapper more effective. As a result of the elasticity in the staves and hoops, the stave will be forced back upward after being struck, but there will be a slight overshot before settling into its final position. Think of this as the resilient stave overshooting a bit then returning to its original position. As the stave moves back down this also creates an additional force to remove the bung. The tapper with a spring handle, if properly used, will bounce up prior to the stave's recoil, and not interfere with the overshot.

Re-coopering

Some of the barrels lasted fifty years or so, but not without occasional repairs. One of the most frequent failures was the bung stave, which had been unintentionally weakened when the bunghole was bored. Sometimes a stave would crack near the chime, and once in a while a hoop required replacing. Cooper Kenneth Kilby writes, "Heads wore the least of all, as they were sunk into each end of a cask and therefore protected..."[12]

Repair work on barrels went on for years after many of the cooperage companies went out of business, becoming the victim of steel and plastic containers.

[1] *Inside the Hoops: A Guide to Better Cooperage*, St. Paul, MN: Northern Cooperage Co., nd, ca. 1942), title page.
[2] Franklin E. Coyne, *The Development of the Cooperage Industry in the United States, 1620-1940* (Chicago: Lumbers Buyers Publishing, 1940). pp. 7, 8.
[3] The author is indebted to E. J. Raimondi for an explanation of this concept that he also applied to examine the robustness of different designs of recessed heads for screws.
[4] Kenneth Kilby, *The Cooper and His Trade* (reprint; 1971, Fresno, CA: Linden Publishing, 1977), p. 24.
[5] Luis Marden, "The Craft of the Cooper," *Colonial Williamsburg Journal*, winter 1998-90, 12: 26. The article was based largely on an interview with George Pettengell, the master cooper in the crafts department.
[6] Coyne, *Cooperage Industry*, p. 36.
[7] Pierre Berton, *Niagara: A History of the Falls* (New York: Penguin Books, 1992), p. 197. Also see Charles Calvin Parish, *Queen of the Mist: The Story of Annie Edson Taylor* (Interlaken, NY: Empire State Books, 1987).
[8] Ibid.
[9] Ibid., p. 202.
[10] As quoted in Coyne, *Cooperage Industry*, p. 36.
[11] F. P. Hankerson, compiler, *The Wooden Barrel Manual* (St. Louis, MO: The Associated Cooperage Industries of America, nd, ca. 1943), p. 45.
[12] Kenneth Kilby, *The Cooper and His Trade,* p. 54.

Chapter 3
The Barrel in Colonial America

John Lewes arrived in Jamestown in January 1608, becoming the first English cooper in America at a permanent settlement. Tight and slack casks for shipping, as well as tubs and buckets for domestic use were in demand by the fledging pioneers, and soon other countrymen with woodworking skills followed. The Virginia Company advertised with broadsides appealing to English coopers and craftsmen to emigrate to Jamestown, offering rewards including small tracts of land. Many paid their own way while others began life in America as indentured servants. These indentures were held for a specific period of time by ship captains, planters and merchants.[1]

In accordance with English law, apprenticeships were legally binding agreements and handled through the courts. Therefore, a written document would have been established between the two parties during the indentured period. One such contract, dated March 15, 1754, reads:

> John Lee Orphan of Thomas Lee is by the Court bound to John Harris til he arrives attains the Age of twenty one years his sd Master is to Learn him to reade and Write and the trade of a cooper and to find and provide him with Sufficient Wholesome & Cleanly Dyet Lodging and Apparell and at the Expiration of his Servitude to pay and allow him as is Appointed for Servants by Indenture or Custome.[2]

Material for staves could be sawed and split from the trees of enormous size found in abundance in Virginia, and throughout most of the east coast. Coopering, however, required the use of sharp iron tools, which were critical to achieving close-fitting parts; hence, water tightness. The settlers observed that Native American had not discovered iron, but nevertheless had developed packaging techniques that depended to a large degree on using grown or found material such as gourds and animal skins for holding their food and belongings. One example provided Thomas Harriot in 1590 is shown in figure 3-1.

Figure 3-1. A "cheefe ladyes" wearing a chain of great pearls, beads of copper, or smooth bones, supports her arm in the ornament, and carries a gourd "full of some kind of pleasant liquor" in her left hand. From Thomas Harriott, *A Brief and True Report of the New Found Land of Virginia* (reprint; 1590, New York: Dover Publications, 1972), page 51.

Stave Exportation

Great Britain, probably the world's greatest naval power during the seventeenth and eighteenth centuries, consumed much of its forest in the construction of ships and in the production of iron. To offset this loss, it was quite natural to turn to America, which was done in several ways. Pig iron, which required great quantities of

THE BARREL IN COLONIAL AMERICA

wood before the introduction of the coke process, was imported. One of the first iron furnaces was established in Cecil County, Maryland at Principio in the early 1700s. England could also purchase sailing vessels directly from the colonies mitigating the drain on their forest. For casks it became logical to import staves, or in some cases "shooks," (being a set of staves, heads and hoops) for a barrel or other container.[3]

Raymond Townsend notes that, "Pipe-staves were manufactured in Virginia as early as 1607."[4] Examining information from about the 1740s, he goes on to observe – when a shipmaster was unable to secure a "full lading of tobacco" he would take on pipe-staves, clapboard and timber. Such exports eventually led to legislation – in February 1752 the Virginia Assembly passed an act to regulate the size of staves and headings being exported to Madeira. Pipe staves were to be four feet, eight inches long, four inches wide and one inch thick. Shorter staves were specified for hogsheads being three feet six inches, four inches wide and three-quarters of an inch thick.

Townsend identified about 300,000 staves being exported by Virginia in 1746, doubling twenty years later to around 600,000 per year between 1763 and 1766. From all the colonies the number was much higher going to 20 million by 1770.[5] Coopers did not necessarily make these, as skilled carpenters and joiners also supplemented their income producing staves for export. Coopers in England and Europe found the American white and red oak to be most satisfactory to produce tight casks.

Tobacco

John Rolfe, who is probably most noted for marrying Pocahontas, is credited with establishing the tobacco trade with England. Learning planting techniques from Native Americans, he developed a way to cure the tobacco for shipment overseas – the first recorded amount was two and one-half thousand pounds exported in 1616 (see figure 3-2). "Although tobacco, in King James' view, was 'loathsome to the eye, hateful to the nose, harmful to the brain' and 'dangerous to the lungs,' it became the mainstay of Virginia and

Maryland economies during the seventeenth and eighteenth centuries . . ."[6]

Tobacco & Snuff of the best quality & flavor,
At the Manufactory, No. 4, Chatham street, near the Gaol
By Peter and George Lorillard,
Where may be had as follows:

Cut tobacco,	Prig or carrot do.
Common kitefoot do.	Maccuba snuff,
Common smoaking do.	Rappee do.
Segars do.	Strasburgh do.
Ladies twift do.	Common rappee do.
Pigtail do. in small rolls,	Scented rappee do. of different kinds,
Plug do.	
Hogtail do.	Scotch do.

The above Tobacco and Snuff will be sold reasonable, and warranted as good as any on the continent. If not found to prove good, any part of it may be returned, if not damaged.

N. B. Proper allowance will be made to those that purchase a quantity.
May 27—tm.

Figure 3-2. A tobacco plant is shown along with a Lorillard advertisement, May 27, 1789, featuring snuff and pipe tobacco. Respectively from E. Benjamin Andrews, *History of the United States*, 6 volumes, (New York: Charles Scribner's Sons, 1915) 1:119, and Alex Groner, *American Business and Industry* (New York: American Heritage, 1972), page 66.

Starting in 1616 with a very modest export, the tobacco trade in the next fifteen years increased by a factor of more than one hundred. It continued to grow up to the time of the American Revolution as seen in table 3-1. Also shown is the estimated number of hogsheads required for export based on the average container holding five hundred pounds.[7]

THE BARREL IN COLONIAL AMERICA

Table 3.1. Tobacco imported by Great Britain during selected years from 1616 to 1775, and approximate number of hogsheads used based on five hundred pound per container.

Year	Pounds of tobacco (thousands)	Number of hogsheads (estimated)
1616	2.5	5
1631	272	544
1669	15,000	30,000
1688	28,000	56,000
1708	30,000	60,000
1730	41,000	82,000
1752	78,000	156,000
1772	97,000	194,000
1775	102,000	204,000

Construction of the hogsheads provided many coopers a steady source of work. Initially the cask produced varied in size and, because many became too large and heavy to be handled, shippers were heard to complain. This appears to be the reason the Virginia Assembly passed a law in 1658 stating:

> [I]ncertainty and extraordinary size of all tobacco caske, which hath bin very much prejudical to them, that a certaine size of all tobacco caske of Virginia hhds. shall be as followeth, vizt, ffourtie three inches in length and the head twentie & six inches wide with the bulge proportioable."[8]

There was a penalty of three thousand pound of tobacco imposed for exceeding this size, or from constructing a hogshead with unseasoned lumber. Nevertheless the problem seemed to continue. Additional legislation was enacted in 1705, adding that persons setting up hogsheads must go before a Justice of the Peace and take an oath of compliance. One problem created by oversized containers can be seen in figure 3-3.

It becomes clear from the mode of transport, the casks had to be very sturdy and constructed in such a way to allow the placement of pins into the head, attaching a frame and thereby making the container into its own wheel. Rolling over primitive trails littered

HISTORY OF THE BARREL IN AMERICA

with stones was punishing on the hogsheads as well as its contents. It was learned that travel more than twenty miles or so did considerable damage to the tobacco, reducing its marketplace value. Around the dock the containers were moved by hand, weighed, and stored in a warehouse until a ship arrived (see figure 3-4).

Figure 3-3. A hogshead of tobacco is shown being pulled by animals along a so-called rolling road en-route to a shipping dock. From Harpers' Weekly, 1869, as found in Ann Finlayson, *Maryland* (Nashville, TN: Thomas Nelson, 1974), page 67.

In the seventeenth and eighteenth centuries, loading containers on ships required strong men to hoist a dockside barrel or hogshead upward while others carefully centered the container over the cargo hatch. It was lowered into the hold below and stowed; the process was reversed when containers were removed from the ship. Through the use of compound rope and tackle the physical lifting effort could be mitigated, but was nevertheless demanding, as shown in figure 3-5. An overstressed hoisting line could break likely causing personal injury and damage to the sailing vessel. So regulating the size, and hence weight of hogsheads, was important.

THE BARREL IN COLONIAL AMERICA

Figure 3-4. An idealized view of a group of wealthy planters discussing business as hogsheads of tobacco are loaded on a ship en-route to Great Britain. From Arthur Pierce Middleton, *Tobacco Coast: A Maritime History of Chesapeake Bay in the Colonial Era* (reprint; 1953, Baltimore: Johns Hopkins Press, 1984), title-page frontispiece.

Figure 3-5. A tobacco hogshead is being held from descending by the man standing at the corner of the hatch. Another man lets the cargo gradually swing to over the cargo hole. From D. H. Montgomery, *The Leading Facts of American History* (Boston: Ginn, 1917), page 50.

HISTORY OF THE BARREL IN AMERICA

Naval Stores

The British government encouraged the American production of important shipboard products consisting of tar, pitch, and turpentine (see figure 3-6). Franklin Coyne notes, "a bounty was granted in 1706 on naval stores exported to England from American colonies and this stimulated trade in this commodity to the extent that there were 9,266 barrels of pitch and tar sent to the mother country in the following year."[9]

Figure 3-6. Barrels of sap from pine trees are rolled up an incline and emptied into the still heated by pine logs. Vapors evaporated are condensed to produce turpentine, and the residue left in the bottom is barreled as pitch or tar depending on its viscosity. From *Scientific American*, October 30, 1880, page 279.

THE BARREL IN COLONIAL AMERICA

Ropes made of hemp were treated with tar to improve water resistance and enhance life, and pitch was used to impregnate hemp that sealed the cracks between the ship planking. Turpentine was much valued in colonial times and employed extensively as a disinfectant, used for washing down the quarters of the crew. This was particularly important for disease control on vessels such as slave ships that transported large groups of people.

Naval stores were initially exported from New England but sometime after about 1760, as the supply of pine trees dwindled because of timbering, much of the production moved into Virginia and the Carolinas. Later it migrated even farther south into Georgia and Florida, where there were large stands of coastal pine. Pine trees were tapped collecting a sticky sap in buckets that was transferred to barrels and transported to nearby turpentine stills like the one shown in figure 3-6.

Townsend reports that the Virginia Assembly in November 1780 moved to control the size of barrels for tar, pitch, and turpentine by putting into law:

> The heads and bulge were to be round, and the heads were not to exceed one inch and a half, nor to be less than one inch thick, the staves were to be of equal length, and not less than three fourths of an inch thick, and no sap-pine timber was to be in the barrels made for turpentine. The barrels were to be well bound with good hoops, at least two thirds of their length, and were to contain thirty-two gallons and a half, wine measure, at least.[10]

Beef and Pork

There was a demand in the Western Islands for beef, pork and other foods that could be raised in America, or in the case of fish, harvested in New England. Imported from islands such as the West Indies were molasses and raw sugar. An indication of the importance of barrels in the transport of such commodities is found in the manifest of one vessel leaving New England with the following cargo:

> 80 hogsheads, 6 barrels and 3 tierces of rum, containing 8,220 gallons; 19 barrels of flour; 4 tierces of rice; 2 barrels of snuff; 20 barrels of tar; 3 barrels of loaf sugar; 7 quarter-casks of wine; 1 barrel of coffee; 1 barrel of vinegar; 20 firkins of tallow; 10 barrels of pork; 15 half-barrels of pork; 4

kegs of pickles; 2 barrels of fish, 1 barrel of hams; 12 casks of bread; 4 casks of tobacco; as well as 3,000 staves, hoops and heading boards.[11]

The Virginia Assembly in the previously mentioned act of November 1780 also included requirements for pork and beef barrels that paralleled the turpentine and tar barrels, but allowed a slight variation of volumes of twenty-nine to thirty-one gallons. Additionally the act specified, "They were to be made of good white oak timber, well seasoned, and clear of sap, and were not to be less than three-fourths of an inch thick; and every cooper or whoever set up any such barrel was to stamp or brand them as directed."[12] No doubt other colonies also enacted similar legislation, as there was a desire for standardization, which can be gleaned from a 1642 order by the Massachusetts Court that read, "that all vessels of casks used in any liquor, fish, or other commodities should be of the London assize, and appointed inspectors to gauge these vessels and mark them with the gauger's mark."[13]

Molasses and Rum

A thriving business existed in parts of New England with the importation of molasses and raw sugar from the West Indies and the production of rum in the distilleries of Boston and in Newport, Rhode Island. This resulted in what has been described as a triangular trade pattern with barrels of rum going to the Gold Coast of Africa, traded for slaves who were transported to the West Indies, then traded for molasses and raw sugar, and finally the vessels sailing to New England.

Before 1700, Newport had twenty-two distilling houses in operation and Massachusetts around that time consumed more the 15,000 hogsheads of molasses annually for the production of rum. Rhode Island's Governor Stephen Hopkins recorded that eighteen ships transported 18,000 hogsheads of rum each year to the Gold Coast. With a demand for thousands of casks, there was ample work for many coopers.[14]

THE BARREL IN COLONIAL AMERICA

Figure 3-7. Edward Teach, better known as Blackbeard, terrorized the American coast during the latter part of the seventeenth and early eighteenth centuries stealing goods, no doubt including kegs of rum. From the Harvard College Library, Harry Elkins Widener Collection, as found in David Budlong Tyler, *The Bay & River Delaware: A Pictorial History* (Cambridge, MD: Cornell Maritime Press, 1955), page 22.

Apple Cider

As apple trees grew well throughout much of the East Coast, the most popular drink among working people was cider, which was made in the fall. An account by Aubrey Land about the diet of planters in Colonial Maryland provides a mention of the beverage:

> The kitchen garden and a few fruit trees met the family needs for fresh fruit and vegetables in season. Many leases specifically required the tenant to

plant and tend a certain number of apple trees. Enterprising housewives dried any surplus against winter months when turnip greens, parsnips or turnips were the only relief from meat and cereal foods until the spring sun brought out Fieldcrest in last year's corn fields. That salad treat of today was the planter's common spring pot herb until still warmer days brought out the poke salat. Cider came nearest being the common beverage of most planting household. Planters, somehow, without cider presses made and consumed many gallons annually.[15]

In 1744, Dr. Alexander Hamilton was traveling through Harford County, Maryland and detained a short while waiting to cross the Susquehanna River on a ferry. The operator provided him with a beverage and he recorded in his dairy, "I drank some of their syder, which was very good."[16]

It is likely many farmers took their apples and barrel containers to nearby water-powered gristmills, some of which also had a cider press. As the farmers were cash poor, a soke system was used in which the miller would retain a portion of the cider for his work in pressing the apples. Later, however, many farmers were able to acquire a small press for their personal use (see figure 3-8).

Figure 3-8. A post-colonial woodcut of an apple press and cider storage barrels is shown. From *Farmers' Almanac, 1980*, (Morristown, NJ: Morris County Savings Bank, 1979), month of October.

Coyne reports, "The making of apple cider was carried on extensively in New England in colonial days. Cider was a favorite drink of the colonist and thousands of barrels were required for the annual output of the presses."[17] He goes on to note that a village of forty families in New England turned out three thousand barrels in

THE BARREL IN COLONIAL AMERICA

1721, while another somewhat larger community produced ten thousand barrels of cider.

Cod Fishing

One hundred and one Pilgrims arrived December 1620 on the *Mayflower* and disembarked at Plymouth, Massachusetts. In this company were only thirty-four grown men, the rest were women and children. It is recorded that one of the men was John Alden, a cooper, who was engaged to bring his skills to America. Later Governor William Bradford would write a history of the Plymouth colony, reporting:

> John Alden was hired for a cowper at South-Hampton, where the ship victuled; and being a hopeful young man, was much desired, but left his own liking to go or stay when he came here; but he stayed, and married here.[18]

Alden probably is not recognized for his woodworking skill, but is best known from Henry Wadsworth Longfellow's narrative poem, *The Courtship of Miles Standish* and winning the hand in marriage of Pricilla Mullins.

Most likely others in the company "were also familiar with the art of coopering, which had been well established in England since Elizabethan days, when guilds of English coopers formed an important part of the trade unions of that time."[19]

The first year in Plymouth was very difficult, with about one half of the company dying during the first six months. For several years there were food shortages, which were exacerbated as more pilgrims arrived. By 1624, a group of pilgrims established a settlement at Cape Ann, but after two years they moved farther south to place called Naumkeag, later named Salem. The arrival of more settlers in 1628 secured the permanency of the location.

Lack of contiguous good farm and pasture land made it difficult to sustain the settlers with adequate food. Fortunately a thirty-eight-year-old minister, Rev. Hugh Peter, led the struggling settlement from the pulpit towards economic security (see figure 3-9). He pointed to the humble cod and also:

HISTORY OF THE BARREL IN AMERICA

[O]rganized the haphazard fisheries, promoted the building of a salt works to process dried fish, and help John Holgrave build a wharf, drying racks or "flakes," and a tavern on Winter Island. Salem fisherman made more ambitious voyages to the rich fishing banks off Cape Cod and Newfoundland, bringing home halibut, mackerel, haddock, and cod.[20]

Figure 3-9. Rev. Hugh Peter (1598-1660) was instrumental in promoting Salem's fishing fleet. On the right is a drying platform for cod. From *Salem: Maritime Salem in the Age of Sail* (Washington, DC: U.S. Department of the Interior, 1987), pages 18 and 21.

The "sacred cod" provided a regular source of food and stabilized the economy, but as the migration of settlers waned around 1637, a surplus of fish threatened their brief security. To get the cod to more distant locations, Rev. Peter encouraged the construction of larger ships, and in 1638 the ship *Desire* returned from the West Indies with a cargo of cotton, tobacco, salt, and slaves. Cod export continued to grow, finding a ready market in the Catholic countries that fasted from meat on Fridays, prompting a French peasant to say, "The codfish is more important than Louis XIV."[21] By 1770, the colonies exported 660,000 quintals or barrels of dried fish, providing steady employment for many coopers.

58

THE BARREL IN COLONIAL AMERICA

Whale Oil

The first whales processed in New England had washed into a shallow area, perhaps as a result of a storm, and were captured to claim their flesh and oil. Native Americans had previously learned of the whale's value and imparted some of their knowledge in processing the mammals to the Puritans. Later, as the demand for oil lighting increased, boats were organized to pursue the whales near the shore (see figure 3-10).

A chance harvesting of a whale off Nantucket Island prompted local residents in 1672 to induce a whaler, James Loper, to come to Nantucket and "Carrey on a Design of Whale catching," where the islanders were to share in one third of the profits. He was to be provided a grant of land and monopoly for two years. In addition, cooper John Savidge, was offered land as an inducement to set up his trade, "as the town or Whale Company have need to employ him."[22]

Whale oil was stored in barrels and, according to Coyne, the coopers who made them "drew more pay than when making the regular run of cooperage."[23] In 1770, whale oil exports from the colonies to Great Britain were 6,667 tons, which required a quantity of about 60,000 barrels.

Figure 3-10. A small boat is shown pursuing a whale to claim it oil, flesh, and bones. From *Scientific American*, April 17, 1880, page 247.

Wheat and Flour

When the colonists arrived in America, one of the first agricultural crops they learned to plant was corn. They discovered, however, fertile soil would support good harvests of wheat and over time this cereal crop became the food of choice. Much of the corn was diverted for animal feed. The Piedmont regions of Virginia and Maryland, as well as large parts of Pennsylvania and western New York, were well suited for growing wheat.

Processing the wheat into flour required several steps. The wheat was passed through grinding stones to produce meal, which had to be cooled and dried before being sifted, or *bolted* as it is called the milling business. Then, the bolting operation separated the outside covering of the wheat kernel, called bran, and the flour was passed to a storage bin for loading into barrels for shipping.

Gristmills built throughout Colonial America were nearly always powered by water, but the milling process was nevertheless very labor intensive. In 1795, Oliver Evans published *The Young Mill-Wright and Miller's Guide,* which described an automated mill where wheat came in one end and flour packed in barrels went out the other. He licensed the invention to hundreds of millers throughout the colonies, and not only was labor significantly reduced, but also the quality of the flour was improved (see figure 3-11).[24]

American flour found a ready market and export from the Port of Baltimore was a major factory in the city's growth. In 1770, flour from the colonies to Great Britain amounted to 45,868 tons, and with each barrel containing 196 pounds net, this corresponded to 468,041 barrels.

THE BARREL IN COLONIAL AMERICA

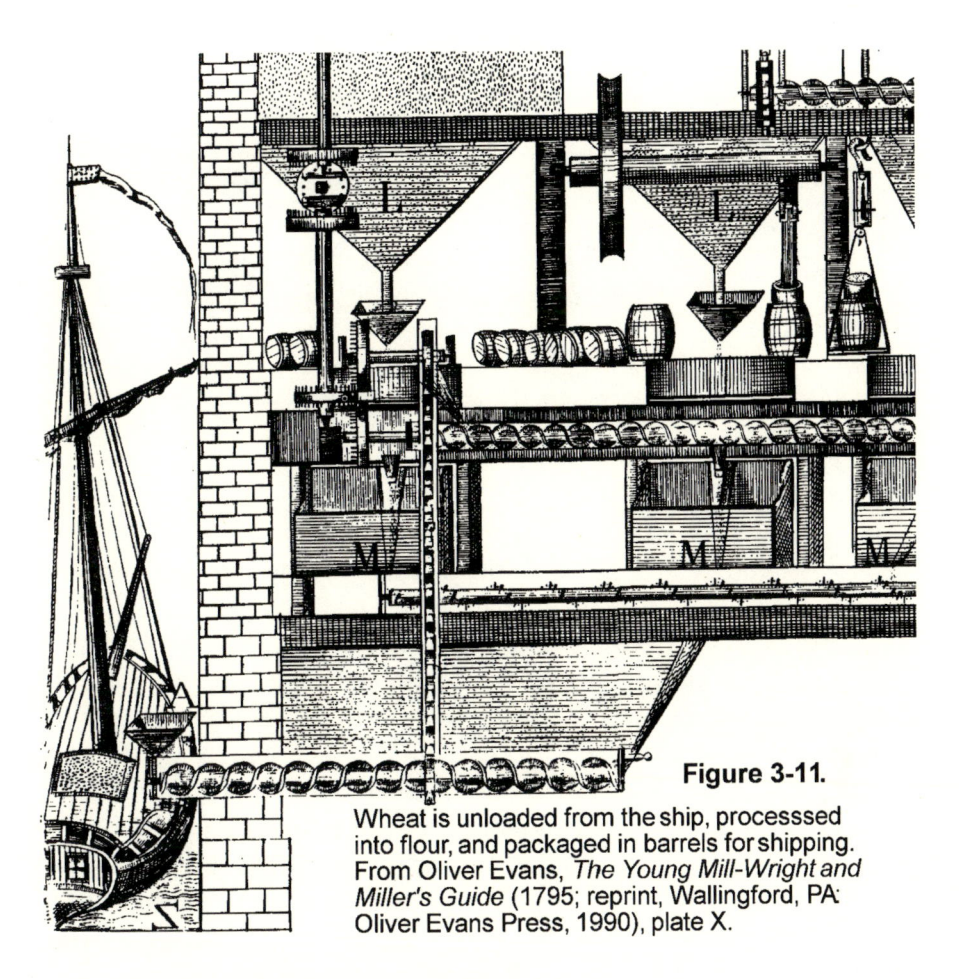

Figure 3-11.
Wheat is unloaded from the ship, processsed into flour, and packaged in barrels for shipping. From Oliver Evans, *The Young Mill-Wright and Miller's Guide* (1795; reprint, Wallingford, PA: Oliver Evans Press, 1990), plate X.

Trade with Native Americans

Animal skins and furs were in high demand in England and parts of Europe, and the Native Americans living in remote areas were skilled hunters and trappers. So it is not surprising English manufactured good were exchanged for these product as shown in figure 3-12.

HISTORY OF THE BARREL IN AMERICA

Figure 3-12. Colonists are shown trading with the Iroquois. From Malcolm Keir, *The March of Commerce* (New Haven, CT: Yale University Press, 1927), page 17.

Revolutionary War

As colonies of Great Britain and protected by perhaps the greatest navy in the world, Americans did not pay much attention to their own defense, save for an occasional Native American uprising. Entrepreneurs were primarily focused on agriculture and trade, while domestic industries such as spinning, weaving, tanning, and candle making provided many of life's necessities. In the case of more technologically advanced products, such as iron foundries, much of the pig iron was shipped to England where it was forged into pots, pans, and other utensils and sold back to the colonists. When war with Great Britain broke out, the country's ports and harbors were unprotected, prompting leaders to develop innovative defenses. One such solution combined barrels with an iron chain (see figure 3-13.

Figure 3-13. Chain barrier supported by wooden barrels is shown at the entrance to the landing at Fort Island, which defended the approach to Philadelphia. From Tyler, *The Bay and River Delaware*, page 33.

THE BARREL IN COLONIAL AMERICA

Domestic Woodenware

Wooden containers were essential for many choirs in everyday Colonial life. Buckets were used to raise water from a well, a churn converted cream into butter, and tubs were used for washing cloths or making soap. In 1975, Historian Brooke Hindle edited a collected group of articles published under the title, *America's Wooden Age: Aspect of its Early Technology.* Perhaps the emphasis on technology precluded a chapter on cooperage and wooden products, but certainly during America's Colonial period, the cooper's output was essential to keeping the family functioning. In addition to containers, some coopers and many handymen made pitchforks, butter molds, and hay rakes used in the home and fields (see several examples in figures 3-14, 3-15, 3-16, and 3-17).

Figure 3-14. Women are shown washing cloths in a wooden tub by sloshing the soapy water around with their feet. From Coyne, *Cooperage Industry*, page 11.

HISTORY OF THE BARREL IN AMERICA

Figure 3-15. A pail which could be used a well bucket. Note the metal bail must be heavy enough to pull the floatable wooden container under water so when raised by a rope it will be full of water. From *Scientific American*, October 23, 1886, page 258.

Figure 3-16 Covered well with a rope over a pulley holding two buckets that are balanced when empty. From Gardner D. Hiscox, *Mechanical Movements: Power and Devices* (1911; reprint, Almonte, Ontario, Canada: Algrove Publishing, 2000), page 143.

THE BARREL IN COLONIAL AMERICA

Figure 3-17. Making soap by boiling fat in a solution of lye. From *Scientific American*, February 18, 1882, page 95.

---

[1] Raymond R. Townsend, "The Cooper in Virginia: Interpretative Notes" (1963?; reprint, Williamsburg, VA: Colonial Williamsburg Foundation Library, 1990) Series 317, pp. 4–5.

[2] Ibid., p. 5.

[3] Barrel staves were found in 1934 from a ship most likely deliberately sunk in 1781 by Cornwallis below Yorktown to prevent a French attack by water. See Ivor Noël Hume, *Here Lies Virginia* (New York: Alfred A. Knopf, 1970), pp. 182–83.

[4] Raymond R. Townsend, "Coopers" (1963; reprint, Williamsburg, VA: Colonial Williamsburg Foundation Library, 1990), Series 316, p. iv.

[5] Ibid, p. vii for the Virginia statistics; and *Historical Statistics for the United States, Colonial Times to 1970*, part 2, pp. 1184–85, table Z 294 for the 1770 figure.

[6] Arthur Pierce Middleton, *Tobacco Coast: A Maritime History of Chesapeake Bay in the Colonial Era* (1953; reprint, Baltimore: Johns Hopkins University Press, 1984), p. 105.

[7] Based on a hogshead holding 500 pounds of tobacco from Robert K. Heinmann, *Tobacco and Americans* (New York: McGraw-Hill, 1960), p. 67. James I. Walsh, "Capacity and Gauge Standards for Barrels and Cask of Early America," *The Chronicle of the Early American Industries Association*, 52: 151, notes, "Maryland changed its capacity assize for tobacco hogsheads at least five times during the 18th century, finally stabilizing the assize at 1,000 pounds."

[8] Townsend, "Coopers," p. vii.

[9] Franklin E. Coyne, *The Development of the Cooperage Industry in the United States, 1620-1940* (Chicago: Lumber Buyers Publishing, 1940), p.12. For an account on the production of turpentine, see C. Malcolm Watkins, "Notes on the Turpentine Industries," *The Chronicle of the Early American Industries Association*, July 1952, 5:25.

[10] Townsend, "Coopers," p. ix.

[11] Coyne, *Cooperage*, p. 11. One may wonder, for example, why there were 10 barrels of pork and also 15 half barrels of pork. Geoffrey M. Footner, author of several books on sailing ships, points out that half barrels filled spaces in the hull that would have otherwise gone unused.

[12] Townsend, "Coopers," p. ix.

[13] Coyne, *Cooperage*, p. 11.

[14] Information for this section dealing with molasses and rum has been primarily derived from Coyne, *Cooperage*, pp. 11–12.

[15] Aubrey C. Land, "The Planters of Colonial Maryland," *Maryland Historical Magazine*, spring, 1972, 67:124.

[16] Christopher Weeks, "Bouncing Along the Post Road: Eighteenth Century Harford County as Seen by Travelers," *Harford Historical Bulletin*, summer, 1993, 57: 85.

[17] Coyne, *Cooperage*, p. 12.

[18] As quoted in ibid., p. 9.

[19] Ibid.

[20] *Salem: Maritime Salem in the Age of Sail*, (Washington, DC: U.S. Department of the Interior, 1987), p. 19.

[21] Coyne, *Cooperage*, p. 10.

[22] George Francis Dow, *Whale Ships and Whaling: A Pictorial History* (1925; reprint, New York: Dover Publications, 1985), pp. 19–20.

[23] Coyne, *Cooperage*, p. 9 (photo caption).

[24] For more information about the Evans automated flourmill, please refer to Eugene S. Ferguson, *Oliver Evans: Inventive Genius of the American Industrial Revolution* (Greenville, DE: The Hagley Museum, 1980), pp. 13–32.

Chapter 4
Making an American Barrel

Types of Cooperage

Cooperage has traditionally been divided into the three general branches: *white*, serving the home and farm markets; *slack* (dry), providing containers for powders, granular products, and dry goods; and *tight* (wet) for holding liquids such as cider, wine, and turpentine. The skill to produce a tight or wet cask has generally been acknowledged to be more difficult, since each stave must closely adjoin its neighbor, and the head must seat and seal snugly in the top and bottom croze or groove.

The white cooper, producing washtubs, buckets, and butter churns, made products for a less physically demanding environment, but nevertheless had to create watertight wooden containers. This branch of cooperage is usually considered to be less skilled than tight containers, but more skilled than slack work.

Most general-purpose wooden shipping containers, however, were of the slack type, holding agriculture commodities such as flour, grain, meat, fish, salt, soap, and beeswax (see Appendix A). A slack cooper, not having to be so exact in fitting often-thinner staves and heads, could produce the casks at a faster rate when compared to tight cooperage.

The word *skill*, however, may not be the best discriminate to differentiate among the three types of cooperage; other factors were considered. For example, the white cooper usually worked in a rural village and provided the inhabitants the wooden items they needed including containers, as well as shovels, hayforks, spoons, and butter molds. Therefore, the villagers represented his primary market and he responded to their needs. To say he was less skilled than a tight cooper may be narrowly defined as accurate for a specific product, say casks, but not true in general, as people and communication skills played a significant role in the white cooper's success.

HISTORY OF THE BARREL IN AMERICA

In many instances, rural areas were not as large as a town or village, perhaps being a hamlet represented by a small cluster of dwellings. In these cases, the population did not support a full-time or part-time cooper, so a traveling cooper sufficed. An individual with his tools on his back, or perhaps going from place to place with a horse and wagon, would stop for a few days in a sparsely populated area, repair wooden items, make new ones as requested, and move on the next location. He was a self-reliant entrepreneur depending to a large degree on his instincts and talents to sustain a living.

Figure 4-1. A nineteenth-century traveling cooper, William Dalley of Turvey. From Kenneth Kilby, *The Village Cooper*, (Great Britain: Shire Publications, 1998), page 2, from an orginal owned by M. S. Longuet-Higgins.

Slack coopers were usually found near a shipping dock, or near some industry that required their products, most likely in an urban setting. Some of these coopers could produce both slack and tight containers, but made a location decision based on family geography or in some cases the ability to earn a higher salary. Many worked on a per piece basis and slack coopers could produce casks at a faster rate, albeit at a lower cost per container as compares to a tight cask, but when adjusted for volume the slack money could be higher.

Likewise, geography was a major factor for the wet cooper. Commercial shippers and industries like breweries and distillers used tight casks and such companies were his principal customers. In the early days of America, the road infrastructure did not provide for easy transport, so being close to point of sale was important. In some

MAKING AN AMERICAN BARREL

instances, the individuals producing tight casks were true artisans, dedicated to their perceived calling to make only the finest containers. In other situations, the urban location coincided with the government seat, providing an opportunity to lobby for and influence legislation favorable to their business.

In any case, however, the tight cooper over time earned a reputation as being the most skilled in his trade. A cask for holding liquids is shown in figure 4-2.

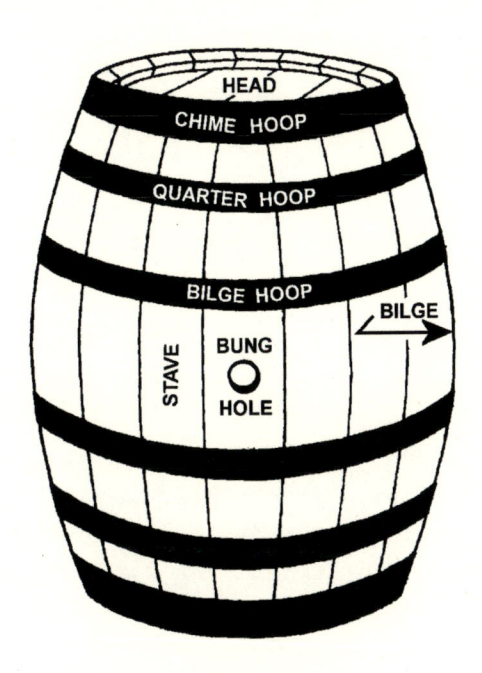

Figure 4-2. A tight barrel consists for three basic parts: (1) a number of staves of varying widths; (2) two heads; and (3) at least four, more often six or even eight hoops. The flared wooden or metal hoops vary in diameter with the chime hoop being wider to protect the ends of the staves. Illustration by the author, 2004.

The Cooper's *Block*

A cooper spent much of his life "at the block"– a short section of an end-standing log firmly imbedded in the ground or attached to the floor, and most likely outfitted on one or more sides with block hooks. Standing here with a broad ax in one hand or a drawknife in both hands, he fashioned the staves for a barrel and other wooden containers (see figure 4-3).

HISTORY OF THE BARREL IN AMERICA

Figure 4-3. Cooper's block. The cooper used the block to trim off wood from the edges of staves to produce the desired barrel shape, and to hold the staves with the hooks while trimming them to the desired curvature. From R A Salaman, *Dictionary of Woodworking Tools,* (1975; reprint, Mendham, NJ: Astragal Press, 1997), page 160.

The early American cooper made a variety of wooden containers that served the diverse needs of his customers, but the tight barrel will be used to describe the essence of skills.

Stave Blanks or Billets

The tight barrel has its origin in the forest at the base of a straight and tall large tree, perhaps two to three feet in diameter. Oak was the preferred wood for tight container because of its toughness and ability to be heated and bent without cracking. The wood, also, in many cases, complemented the taste of stored wine and distilled spirits.

The early American cooper may have been involved in securing oak timber, but more likely less-skilled lumbermen would fell the tree and cut the trunk into lengths called *bolts*, slightly longer than the required staves. Depending on the size of the tree, the bolts may be too heavy to be handled by a two- to three-man crew, so using wedges and sledge hammers the bolts would be split into quarters, loaded onto a wagon or skid, and transported to a location where they would be further split into rough staves or blanks (see figures 4-4 and 4-5).

MAKING AN AMERICAN BARREL

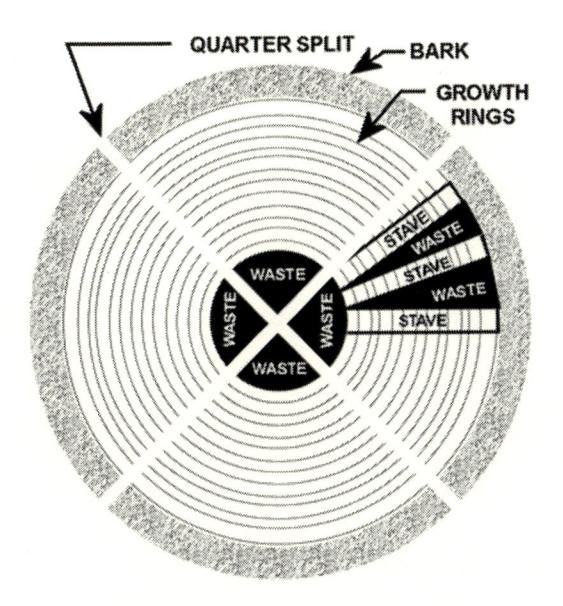

Figure 4-4. Cross-section of a bolt shown quartered and how rough staves, or blanks, would be split out with a froe. The outside portions labeled "waste" could be further split into blanks of a narrower width. Illustration by the author, 2004.

Splitting green white oak with a froe or fromard can be done fairly easily if the wood has no knots. The woodsman holds the froe in one hand by its upright handle and drives the back of the blade with a wooden club. Once driven in, the handle on the froe is pulled forward or pushed back to cause a blank to split off (see figure 4-5).

Figure 4-5. A cooper or woodsman splits a blank from a quartered section of an oak tree using a froe or fromard and a wooden mallet. Illustrations by William T. Sisson, 2004.

71

Before the cooper could use the blanks, they had to be air-dried for several months, and this was done by arranging them crisscrossed in stacks four to five feet high in a yard usually near the cooperage. As the oak dissipated moisture, the widths of the blanks would decrease about eight percent. The lengths, however, barely change, shortening only one-tenth to three-tenths percent. Drying was important, since shrinkage in the width of the wood after a barrel was made would produce cracks between the staves and obviously leaks.

Listing the Stave

After drying, or seasoning as the process is sometimes called, the blanks were delivered to the cooperage. Constructing a barrel begins with the cooper selecting a set of blanks and pieces for the heads, which when properly shaped, will produce a barrel of the desired size. If, during the seasoning, a slight warp occurs in an otherwise satisfactory blank, this is corrected by the cooper through a process known as *dressing* by the use of a straightedge drawknife.

The next step is to *list* the blank with a broad ax that has a handle offset from the cutting edge by perhaps one inch. This allows the cooper to taper the sides of the blanks without having the handle obscure his view of the cutting edge, and equally importantly, positioning his hand gripping the handle away from the side of the blank, thereby avoiding physical interference during the strike. It has been suggested that skilled individuals worked with such precision during listing that: "Some [English] coopers could boast of being able to lay a silk handkerchief on their block and list a set of staves without so much cutting the silk." An exaggeration? Perhaps, but no doubt the coopers swung the ax with an accuracy that, save a few, does not exist in the hand of an individual today (see figure 4-6).

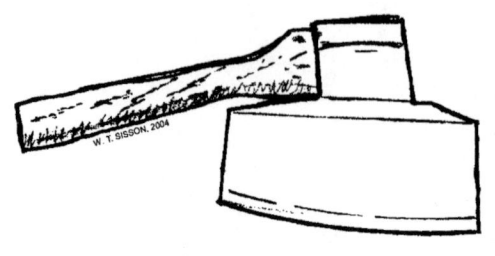

Figure 4-6. Short-handled broad ax with an offset handle used to list a stave. Illustration by William T. Sisson, 2004.

MAKING AN AMERICAN BARREL

The amount of wood listed or removed from the blank directly impacted the bulge in the barrel. A tight fish-bait barrel used today by the Nova Scotia lobster fleet holds 30 gallons and has a bilge-to-head ratio of 1.14:1 (see Chapter 7). This would require about seven percent of each edge be chopped away at the ends, gradually tapering to near zero at the center of the blank (see figure 4-7).

Next it is necessary to shape the blank on both the inside and outside to form a small segment of a circle. This is done by the cooper placing one end into the jaw of a stave or block hook (see figure 4-8), using his mid-section, protected by an apron, to lock the blank in place, and using a backing knife (drawknife) shave the wood from the backsides to produce the outside of the circle.

Figure 4-7. Rough stave or blank shown with dashed lines indicating the portion listed by the broad ax. Illustration by the author, 2004.

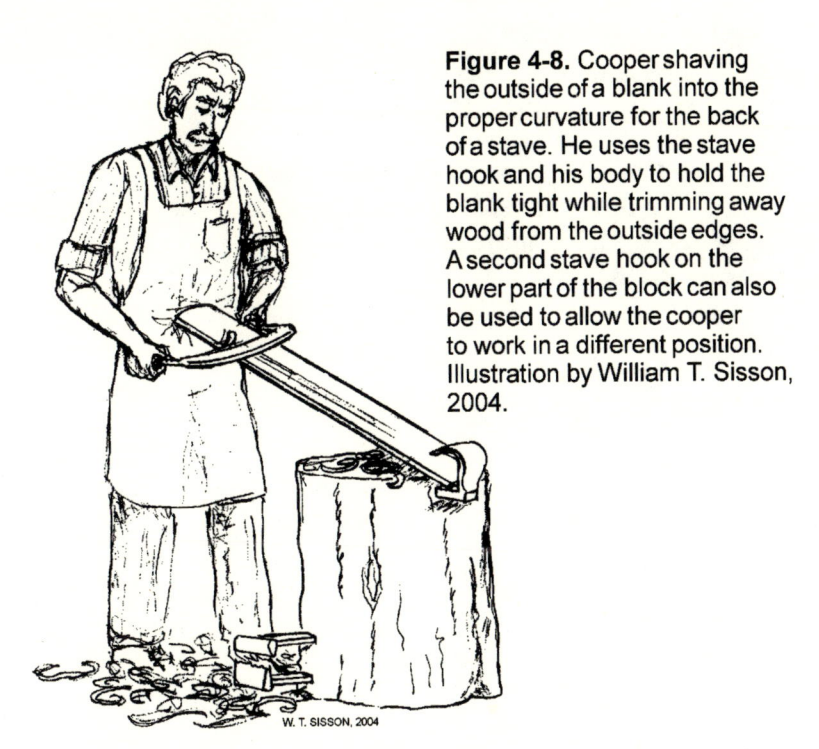

Figure 4-8. Cooper shaving the outside of a blank into the proper curvature for the back of a stave. He uses the stave hook and his body to hold the blank tight while trimming away wood from the outside edges. A second stave hook on the lower part of the block can also be used to allow the cooper to work in a different position. Illustration by William T. Sisson, 2004.

The backing knife usually had a straight blade,[1] however, one old tool catalog depicted a drawknife or backing shave with a blade slightly curved toward the user (see figure 4-9). After rounding off about one half of the length on each side, the blank is rotated, clamping the other end. The remaining portion is similarly prepared.

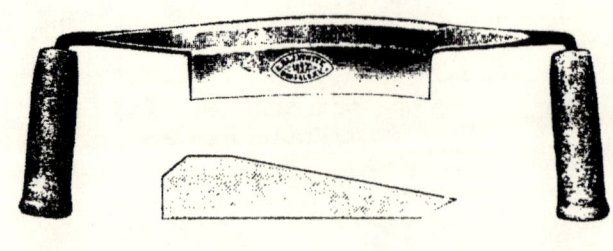

Figure 4-9. Backing shave. From Cope, page 186.

The blank is turned over and a hollowing knife (see figure 4-10) is used to remove wood from the inside of the stave.

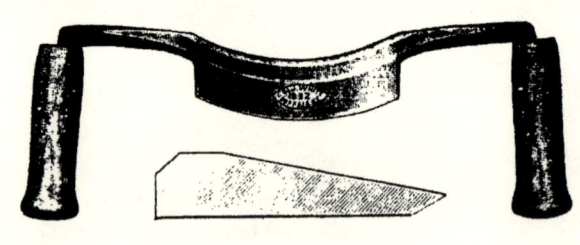

Figure 4-10. Hollowing shave. From Cope, page 187.

While the back of the stave was trimmed its entire length, journeyman cooper Marshall Scheetz notes, "The inside ends or *shoulders* of the stave are left un-hollowed," making them stronger after the croze is cut for the head (see figure 4-11).[2]

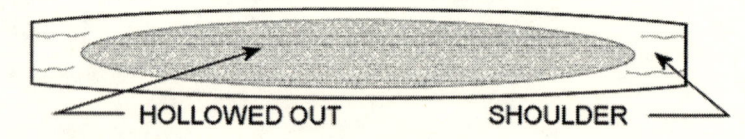

Figure 4-11. Hollowing is done on the inside of a stave to make it easier to bend once heated. Illustration by the author, 2004.

Thus far, all of the work in stave preparation has been done "at the block," although when preparing short staves for a bucket, firkin, or piggin, some coopers prefer to work at a shaving horse. This is a foot-operated vice, which allowed the cooper to sit at one end and

MAKING AN AMERICAN BARREL

position a stave in front of him, held on the opposite end clamped in the jaws of the shaving horse (see figure 4-12).

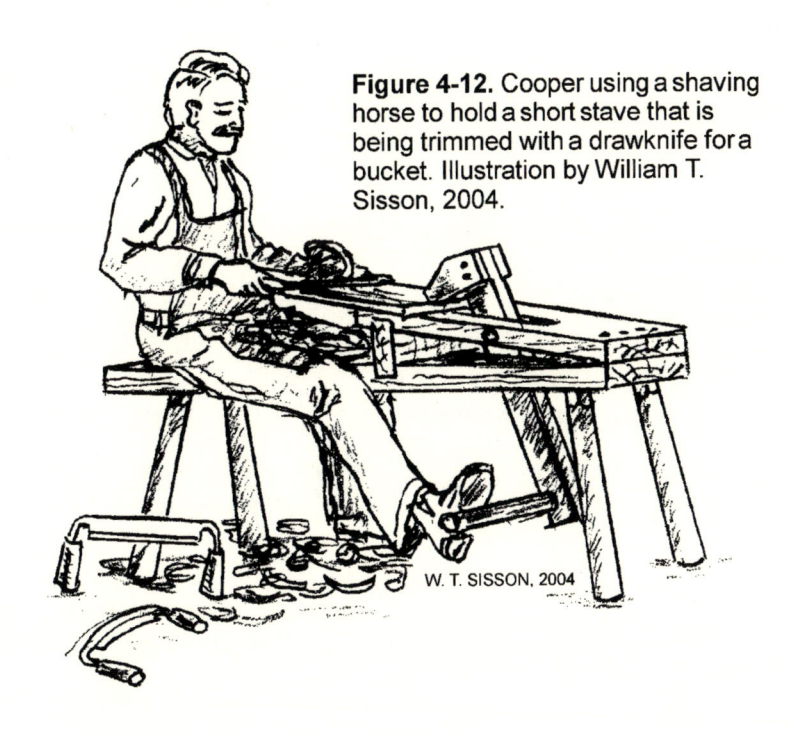

Figure 4-12. Cooper using a shaving horse to hold a short stave that is being trimmed with a drawknife for a bucket. Illustration by William T. Sisson, 2004.

Putting the *Shot* on the Stave

Once the blank is prepared, an angle or *shot* is cut on each edge that is directly related to the number of staves that make up a barrel. A larger number of staves, N, requires a smaller angle (in degrees) as reflected in the formula: angle = 90 − 90(N-2)/N. As examples, a small tub with six staves would be a 30-degree angle; a barrel with eighteen staves, would be a 10-degree angle.

Implicit in this formula, however, are two variables that render it ineffective for the cooper. First, the number of staves cannot be known ahead of time because individual stave widths vary; and second, because widths vary, the angle between adjacent staves must be adjusted. "During the apprenticeship," Scheetz notes, "the cooper is taught to judge angles by eye depending on the varied width of the staves. You are taught this because it is the most efficient way for producing cooperage."[3]

HISTORY OF THE BARREL IN AMERICA

The angle is cut on a cooper's joiner, which is a wooden block plane several feet long, turned upside down, and propped up on one end (see figure 4-13). It can be leaned against something sturdy like the block or the beak iron, or the raised end may be firmly wedged against anything that is stable. The cooper holds the stave at the desired angle or shot and pushes it downward across the blade, being careful to slightly guide the listed edge to produce a short section of a large circle. Depending how well the stave has been listed with the broad ax, usually more than one pass over the joiner is necessary. Scheetz says the cooper judges this by the feel and the sound made by the thin strip of wood being removed by the blade, "as well as continually stopping to judge by eye."[4]

Figure 4-13. Cooper's joiner is used to cut the angle on both edges of a stave. The three-to-six-foot long plane was mounted upside down, propped up on one end, and the stave guided down and over the center-mounted blade. From Cope, page 167.

The process continues until the cooper is satisfied the stave is properly listed. But it is possible, Scheetz notes, "You will have to readjust the shot later."[5]

The oak wood produces a wonderful aroma that is unique to a cooperage, and the strips can be gathered up to fuel a cresset for heating a barrel prior to trussing. At least one English cooper found another use for the strips. "Old Sam Kilby used to write an IOU on a jointer shaving"[6] sending it by one of his men to a pub for a jug of beer.[7]

The steps in dressing a blank stave are shown in figure 4-14. First, with a straight-edged drawknife "square up" a blank that may have slightly warped during the drying process. Second, list the taper on both edges of the blank with a cooper's ax. Third, round the outside of the blank with a drawknife called a backing shave. Fourth, hog out the inside of the blank with a hollowing shave. Fifth, run the blank over a joiner, producing the angle that is appropriate.

MAKING AN AMERICAN BARREL

Figure 4-14. Steps in dressing a rough stave or blank into a finished stave for use in a barrel. Shown are the end views with tree growth rings indicated by the slightly curved vertical lines. The straight lines on both ends represent the edge of the listed portion. Illustration by the author, 2004.

A. Quarter split rough barrel stave.

B. Stave listed on both ends for taper.

C. Stave rounded on top with draw knife.

D. Rounded on bottom with hollowing shave.

E. Stave after running through the joiner.

Raising the Barrel

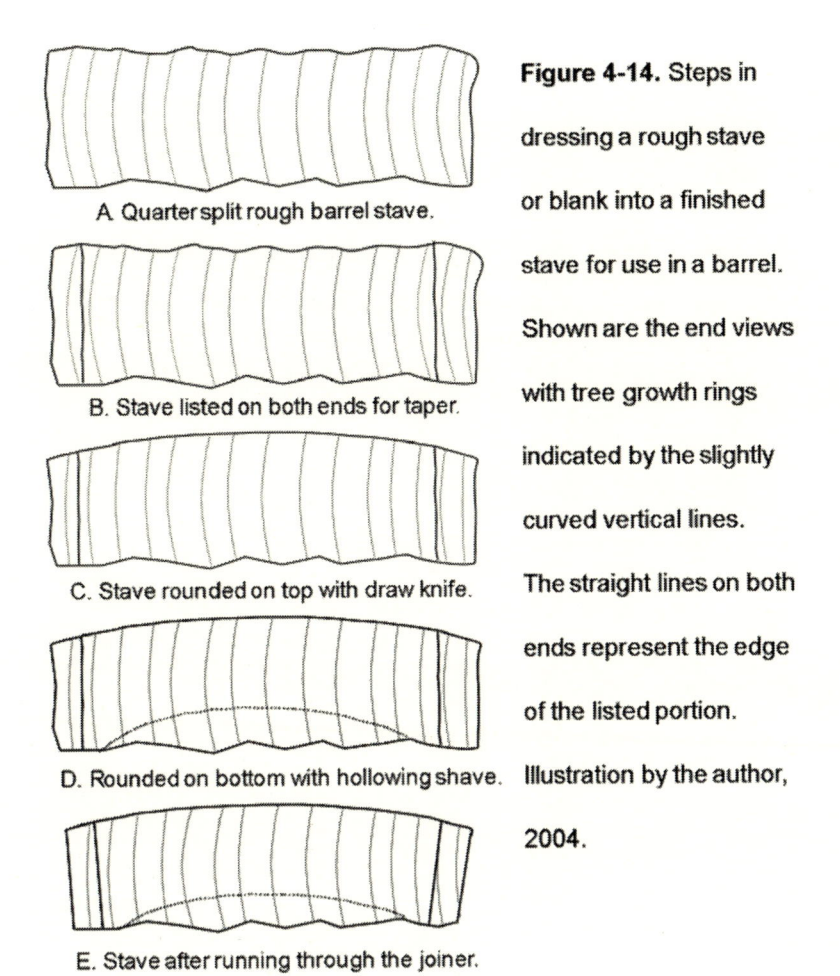

Raising the barrel requires significant skill and a bit of preplanning. The cooper stands with slightly bent knees leaning over a *raising hoop* and a stack of staves (see figure 4-15).

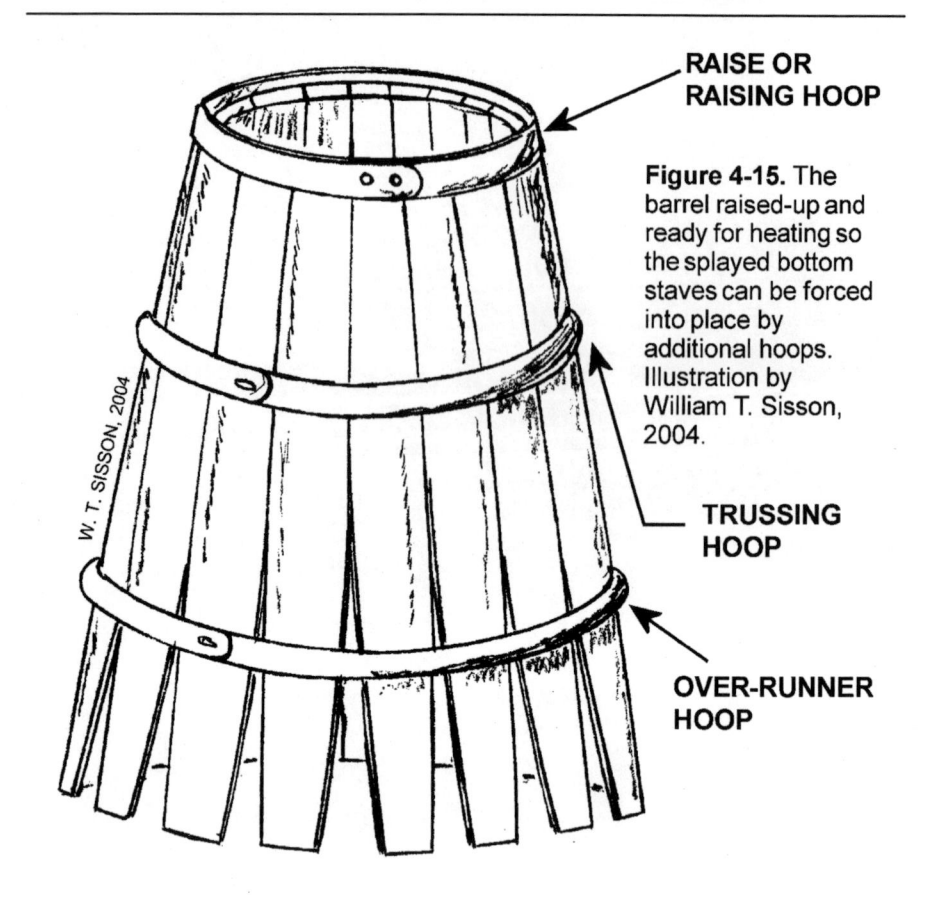

HISTORY OF THE BARREL IN AMERICA

Figure 4-15. The barrel raised-up and ready for heating so the splayed bottom staves can be forced into place by additional hoops. Illustration by William T. Sisson, 2004.

Labels: RAISE OR RAISING HOOP; TRUSSING HOOP; OVER-RUNNER HOOP

Initially the end-standing staves are cradled against his leather apron, supported by slightly separated knees. He holds a raising hoop horizontally at the proper height in one hand and with the other starts to arrange each stave side-by-side using one knee to help support the loose staves. A problem can occur if the last stave is too narrow or wide to complete the top circle. At this point, he may have to remove one or more staves and find a combination that closes with the desired circumference.

Once the last stave is in place, the hoop can be pressed down, first by hand, and then driven with a hammer to draw the tops of the staves tightly together. A second larger *trussing* hoop is then placed to draw the sides of the staves together, and a third still larger hoop, called an *over-runner*, is forced down slightly to gather the staves at the opposite end.

MAKING AN AMERICAN BARREL

Wood chips from the joiner and from listing the staves are packed fairly tightly into an open metal basket called a cresset (see figure 4-16). If the chips are not arranged properly, they can burn unevenly or too fast and not last the twenty to thirty minutes or so necessary to completely heat the barrel to make the staves pliable enough to bend. Once properly fueled, the upper most part of the woods chips are lit.

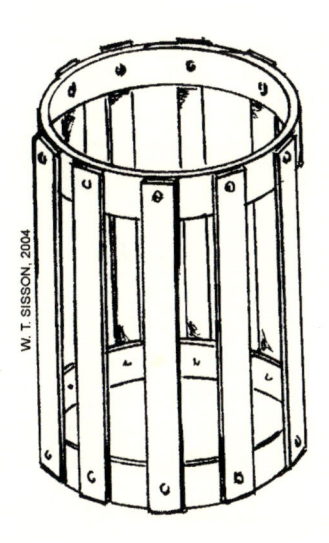

Figure 4-16. Cresset for holding wood chips to heat a barrel to allow the staves to be bent into shape. It is often made from short pieces of metal hoop material riveted together being about eight inches in diameter and twelve inches high. Illustration by William T. Sisson, 2004.

The raised-up barrel, called a "gun," is placed over the cresset and the inside is heated to make the staves pliable enough to be trussed into shape. The aroma emanating from the heated barrel is described as very pleasant. Kilby notes, "Ask any cooper to tell you what constitutes the most agreeable, the most captivating smell and he'll tell you it is the smell of a cask immediately after it has been fired. The piping-hot oak gives off an aroma like that of a richly spiced cake being baked."[8]

After twenty to thirty minutes, the barrel is hot and pliable enough to be trussed. This requires the work of more than one individual, and in accordance with British tradition, the cooper would cry out "truss oh!" and his apprentice or another cooper would assist in forcing the splayed staves together by driving additional trussing hoops into place. The cask finally assumes its traditional barrel shape, now called a "case." To cause the bent staves to take a "set," the case

HISTORY OF THE BARREL IN AMERICA

is again placed over the cresset and is covered with a "pompey" lid to create an oven. After an additional heating, most of the springiness in the bent staves will be relieved, and they will generally retain the barrel shape even after a hoop is removed.

Preparing the "Case" for the Heads

The cooper removes the case from the fire and drives the raising hoop just below the ends of the staves. He uses a short-handle adz to trim off the ends of the staves to the same length, a process known as leveling, and also bevels the inside edge to produce the chime (see figure 4-17). This procedure is repeated for the other end. After this, the ends of the staves at the top of the chime are smoothed off with a topping plane (see figure 4-18). To make the cutting easier, this is done while the wood is still warm and a bit pliable.

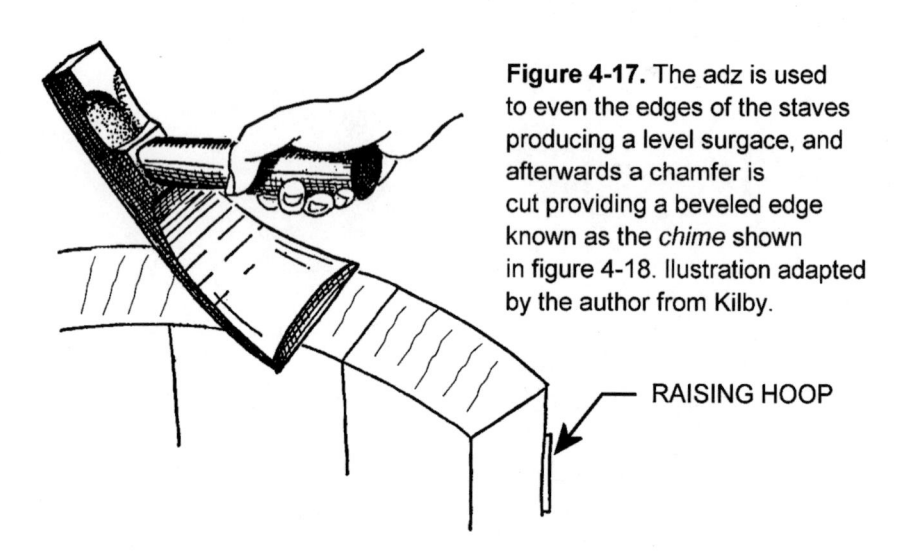

Figure 4-17. The adz is used to even the edges of the staves producing a level surgace, and afterwards a chamfer is cut providing a beveled edge known as the *chime* shown in figure 4-18. Ilustration adapted by the author from Kilby.

RAISING HOOP

The insides of the barrel at the top and bottom are very uneven because of the unprepared shoulder on the end of the staves (refer back to figure 4-13E). To install a circular head, it is first necessary to prepare a smooth inside band close to the top with a tool known in America as a howel plane (in England it's known as a chiv), shown in figure 4-19. The plane is used inside the barrel, being positioned a short distance from the top by a wooden guide attached

MAKING AN AMERICAN BARREL

to it. The face of the plane is curved to fit snugly against the inside the barrel, and with a concave cutting blade, produces a shallow two-inch-wide channel known as the howel, just below the chime.

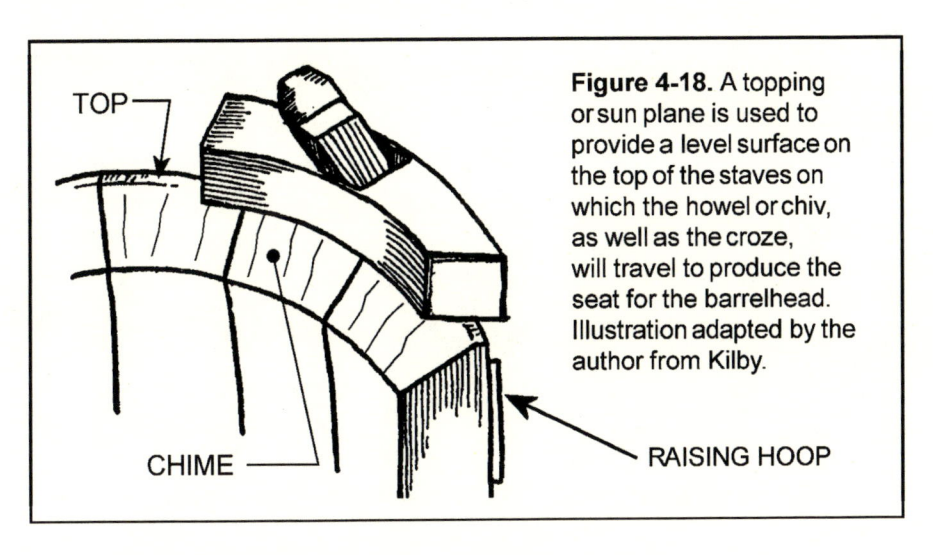

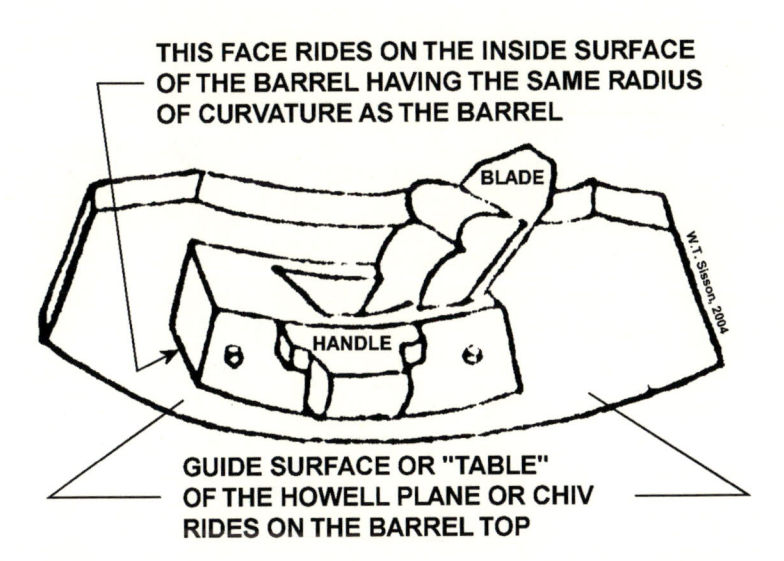

Figure 4-18. A topping or sun plane is used to provide a level surface on the top of the staves on which the howel or chiv, as well as the croze, will travel to produce the seat for the barrelhead. Illustration adapted by the author from Kilby.

Figure 4-19. A chiv or howel plane has a curved blade that cuts an even concave groove around the inside of the barrel to form a shallow channel into which the croze can be cut. Illustration by William T. Sisson, 2004.

HISTORY OF THE BARREL IN AMERICA

The next step is to cut the croze that will accept the barrelhead. This is done with a routing croze plane, which appears similar to the howel plane, but has a single narrow cutting blade, which fashions a datto-like groove. When the operation is finished, the staves have the cross-section shown in figure 4-20. When properly configured, the "bite" of the head will completely fill the croze making contact in three places, on both edges and in the bottom of the croze. This provides for three points of seal for the barrelhead.

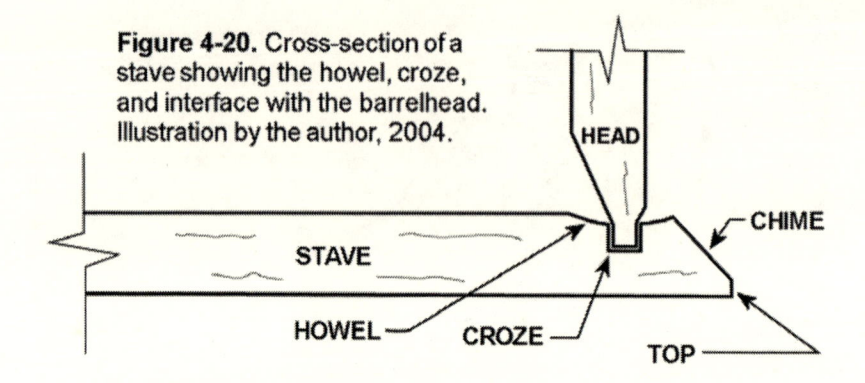

Figure 4-20. Cross-section of a stave showing the howel, croze, and interface with the barrelhead. Illustration by the author, 2004.

Making the Barrelheads

Before the heads can be sawed to their proper size, it is necessary to measure the diameter of the croze, which has been cut into both ends of the barrel. This is done with a compass using trial and error. Points are set a distance apart that approximates the head's radius and the compass is stepped around the inside of the croze until the distance between the points becomes exactly one-sixth of the circumference. This procedure precisely determines the radius of the head, as can be seen from figure 4-21.

The head is constructed from two or more pieces of rectangular wood joined with dowels and sealed between the pieces with strips of a dried reed known by the cooper as *flags*. When the barrelhead is installed the boards are squeezed together and the flag compresses, and upon contact with a liquid inside the barrel, the dried reed swells, ensuring the joints between the boards will not leak.

MAKING AN AMERICAN BARREL

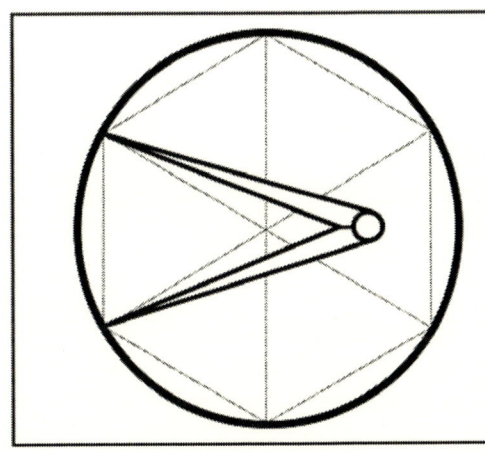

Figure 4-21. Through a trial and error procedure the compass points are adjusted to close on six steps around the croze. Note the six inscribed equilateral triangles prove the validity of such a technique for determining the radius of the barrelheads. Illustration by the author, 2004.

Prior to assembly, each piece of headstock is dressed to the proper thickness with a drawknife (heading knife), and the edges are passed over the joiner. Once dowelled together, the head is sawed out using a bow saw, and a combination of broad ax and knife is used to shape the edge of the head so it will snugly fit into the croze (see figure 4-22). The surface of the head may be further smoothed with a two-handed plane known as a *heading swift* (see figure 4-23).

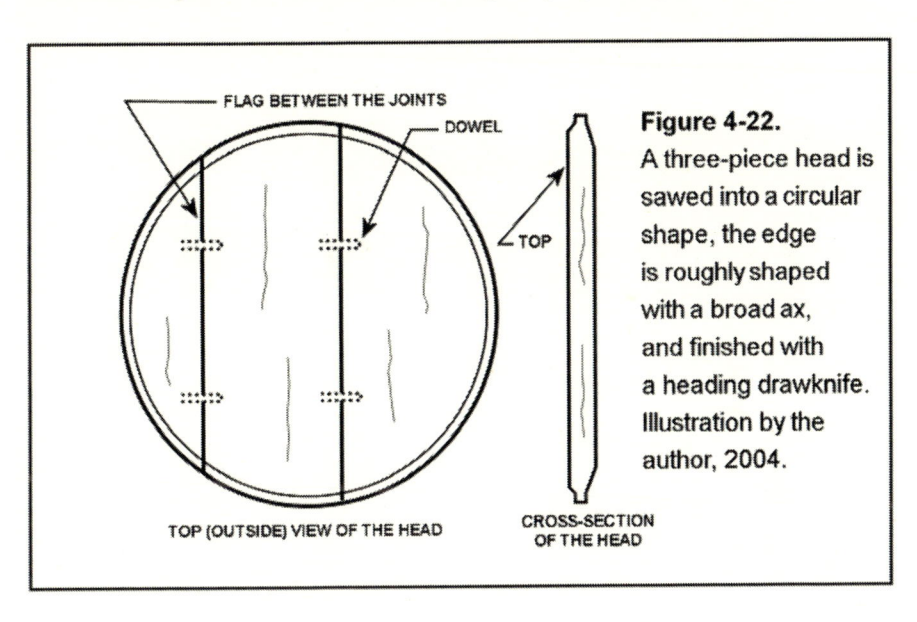

Figure 4-22. A three-piece head is sawed into a circular shape, the edge is roughly shaped with a broad ax, and finished with a heading drawknife. Illustration by the author, 2004.

83

HISTORY OF THE BARREL IN AMERICA

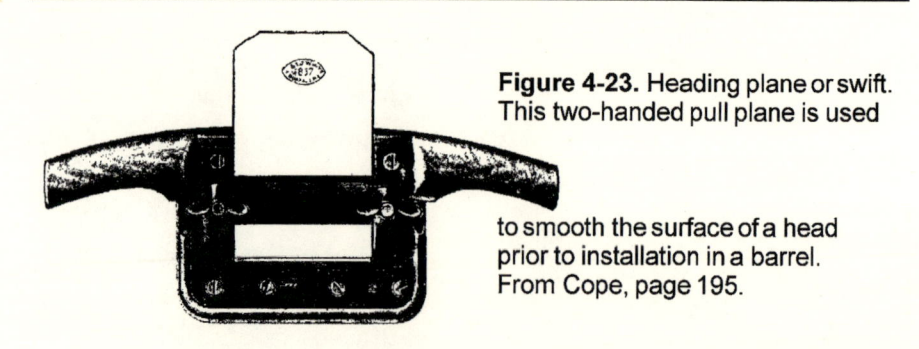

Figure 4-23. Heading plane or swift. This two-handed pull plane is used to smooth the surface of a head prior to installation in a barrel. From Cope, page 195.

"Cleaning Down"

The case is now topped, howled and crozed, but before the heads are installed the barrel is cleaned inside. In general, there are small discontinuities at the joints because of minor differences in the thickness of staves, as well as, rough spots that need to be dressed to mitigate the adhesion of foreign material inside. Scheetz also notes this would be the appropriate time to remove soot and buildup from the trussing (firing). Two of the scraping tools employed to clean the inside and one to smooth the outside are shown in figure 4-24.

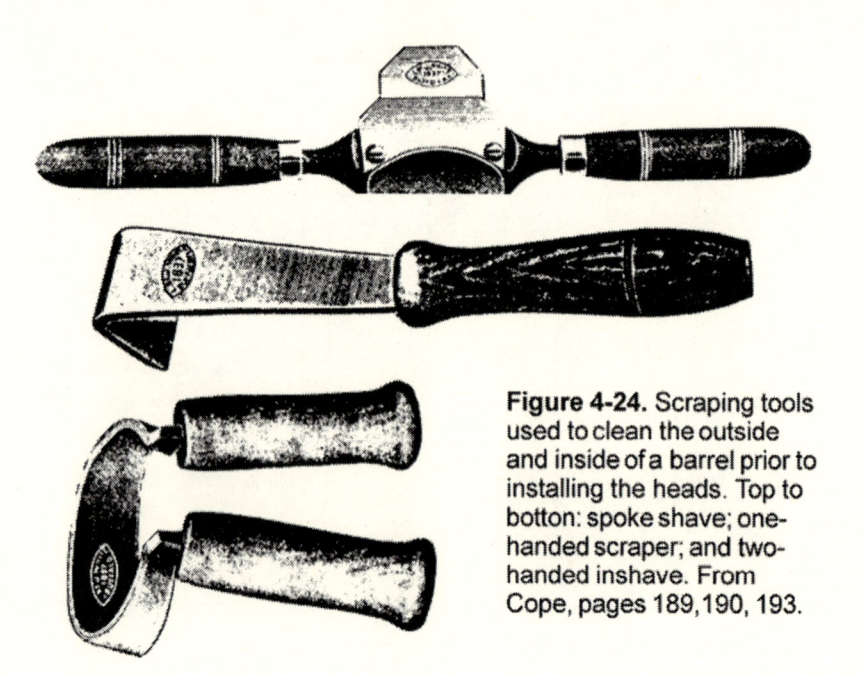

Figure 4-24. Scraping tools used to clean the outside and inside of a barrel prior to installing the heads. Top to bottom: spoke shave; one-handed scraper; and two-handed inshave. From Cope, pages 189, 190, 193.

MAKING AN AMERICAN BARREL

Installing the Heads and Hoops

The raising hoop is removed on one end and the bilge (trussing) hoop is loosened so the staves open slightly. The head is positioned with its edge perpendicular to the end of the barrel and slipped inside toward the bilge. From the opposite end the head is pushed into the croze. The procedure is repeated on the other end, but in this case a screw-tipped metal rod with a handle attached, called a *thief* or *heading vice*, is used to pull the head back up into the croze.[9]

Once the heads are installed, the final chime hoops are put into place to draw the ends of the staves tightly against the head. Scheetz notes, "Then you buzz the outside surface of the cask so it is even. Mainly this is important where two staves meet at a point, as the hoop will not provide even tension if the joint is uneven between the staves." (See figure 4-23 for two-handed draw plane that is similar to a cooper's buzz.) After this, the remaining four hoops (see figure 4-2) are installed to ensure all the staves are tightly pressed together.

If the hoops are made of iron, they are first prepared by attaching the ends of the strips together with rivets, done on a small cooper's anvil, called a beak horn or beak iron (see figure 4-25).

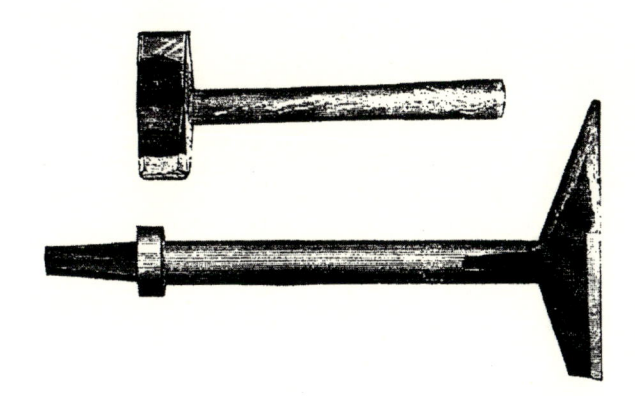

Figure 4-25. Cooper's hammer and anvil or beak iron used for preparing metal hoops. The anvil is mounted upright in a block of wood. From Cope, page 148.

Once proper size hoops are made, and flared on one side to match the curvature of the barrel, they are installed. To force them into position, the cooper used a hoop driver and hammer (see figure 4-26).

HISTORY OF THE BARREL IN AMERICA

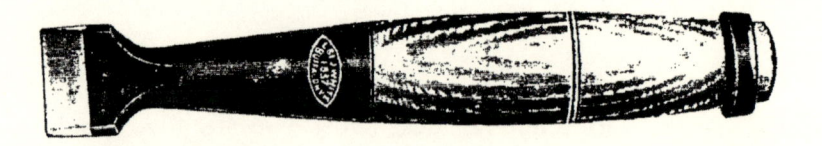

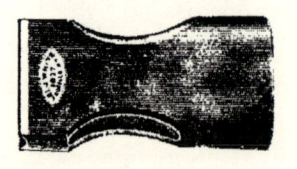

Figure 4-26. On the top is a steel driver with a wooden handle for driving wooden hoops. On the bottom is a steel driver (handle not shown) for securing metal hoops. Note the U-groove in the face. From Cope, pages 190 and 191.

The driver, which may have a concave head to catch the hoop, is placed alongside the barrel on the edge of a hoop and hit with a four to six pound hammer. The cooper works his way around the hoop, keeping it approximately level as it is pounded into place. If wooden hoops are used, the driver is also made of wood.

After installing the last hoop, the cooper checks the barrel to determine its tightness by tapping on the container with a hammer. A tight cask will resonate with a distinctive echo that the discerning ear of the cooper will eagerly detect. If necessary, the hoops will be driven tighter, rechecked, and the barrel will be marked or signed by the cooper. In some cases, the customer may have requested some portion of the barrel be painted or otherwise labeled to indicate its owner.

A bunghole is usually bored through the widest, hence, most likely, the strongest stave, but Scheetz points out, "Boring a bung and filling the cask was traditionally not done by the cooper, but by the brewer or vintner at the brewery or winery."[10] The tip of the auger pulls the cutter into the wood, making a hole, which is enlarged by continued rotation of the conical cylinder with a knife cutting edge (see figure 4-27). This rotation is continued until the desired diameter is achieved. Thereafter, the inside of the hole is sometimes burnished with a hot iron to "seal" the wood, which some coopers said enhances the life of the hole and of the stave.

MAKING AN AMERICAN BARREL

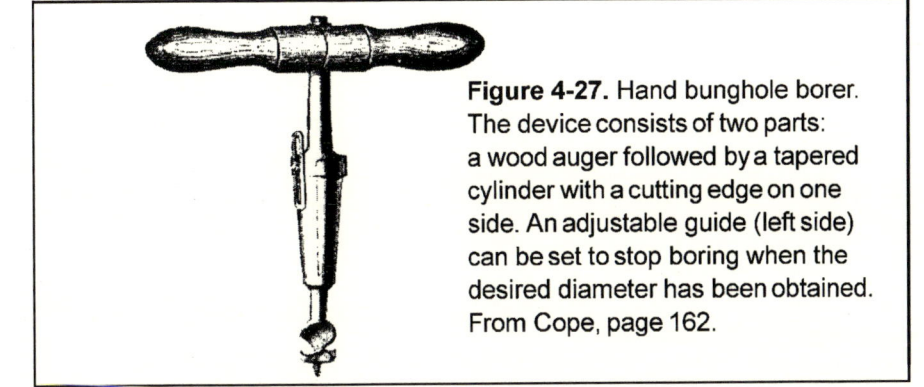

Figure 4-27. Hand bunghole borer. The device consists of two parts: a wood auger followed by a tapered cylinder with a cutting edge on one side. An adjustable guide (left side) can be set to stop boring when the desired diameter has been obtained. From Cope, page 162.

Clothing and Tools

Most coopers wore a leather apron to protect clothing against the rough edges of the wooden containers. The thick covering also allowed work to progress in a more comfortable manner. If wooden rings were used for trussing or for the final hoops, they required chalking on the inside to keep them from popping out of place, so the apron most likely would have a pocket for the chalk.

The cooper's tools rested on a shelf close to where his work was accomplished. If a shaving knife or adz became dull, the physical effort to complete a task would increase and the quality of the finished product would suffer. Therefore, always close by was a sharpening stone to produce "keen" edges on the tools. As most honing materials were called "oil stones," they worked better when lubricated with a small amount of linseed oil, which was also used on the bottom of planes and on the joiner to allow the tools to "sympathize with the wood." See figure 4-28.

Figure 4-28. Oilstone or whetstone used to sharpen steel tools. It is shown in a wooden box. From R. A. Salaman, *Dictionary of Woodworking Tools* (1975; reprint, Mendham, NJ: Astragal Press, 1997), page 285.

HISTORY OF THE BARREL IN AMERICA

Summary

The cooper was a very skilled and respected member of his community, and his products were in great demand. He often performed difficult tasks in a noisy and smoky environment, constructing many sturdy containers each day. For hundreds of years the robust barrels he produced facilitated the movement of population-sustaining products and protected the contents against adulteration.

---

[1] Observation by Marshall Scheetz, journeyman cooper for the Colonial Williamsburg Foundation in Williamsburg, VA, made in a correspondence with the author on Dec. 1, 2004.
[2] Ibid.
[3] Ibid.
[4] Ibid and interview with Marshall Scheetz on June 26, 2004 in Williamsburg, VA.
[5] Scheetz, correspondence.
[6] Kenneth Kilby, *The Cooper and His Trade* (reprint; 1971, Fresno, CA, Linden Publishing, 1977), p. 24.
[7] The author from his youth recalls the pleasant aroma of strips being planed from a piece of wood by his father. The smell is indeed unique to the specie of tree.
[8] Kenneth Kilby, *The Cooper*, p. 28
[9] Scheetz provided this head installation procedure to the author in a correspondence.
[10] Scheetz, correspondence.

Chapter 5
America Barrels Along

After the Revolutionary War, American trade with Great Britain and the European continent increased, bringing wealth to many shippers. Getting American goods from the East Coast to foreign ports was relatively straight forward, but producers in the western part of the country depended on floating them down the Ohio and Mississippi rivers to New Orleans (see figure 5-1).

Figure 5-1. Flatboat with barrels of goods and other products aboard is floated down the Mississippi River to New Orleans where they were sold. The boat was disassembled into lumber, which was also put into the market. From William H. Mace, *A School History of the United States* (Chicago: Rand McNally, 1905), page 217.

Land west of the Mississippi belonged to Spain and through a treaty with the United States, Americans had the "right of deposit," that is, to store good at New Orleans for export. In 1800, however, Spain secretly transferred her American holdings to France, and two years later, before the formal transfer had taken place, the Spanish governor revoked the American "deposit right." This greatly alarmed the West, and President Thomas Jefferson soon found a remedy with the Louisiana Purchase from France in 1803 (see figure 5-2).

HISTORY OF THE BARREL IN AMERICA

Figure 5-2. Thomas Jefferson was president of the United States during the Louisiana Purchase. In November 1810, he wrote in his *Farm Book*, "a cooper's task is 4. flour barrels a day from the rough, i.e. from stuff merely rived out into thickness for 2. staves. and 6. barrels a day when the staves are drawn." Image from Mace, page 200; quote from www.thomasjeffersonpapers.org/farm., October 3, 2004.

The Embargo Act

During the early part of the 1800s, England and France were at war, but Americans traded with both parties. In 1805, however, Great Britain issued a decree closing some continental ports to disadvantage France, and Napoleon retaliated by forbidding France and her allies from trading with the British.

England began stopping vessels, looking for British sailors who would be seized and force to serve in their navy. In 1807, the American ship *Chesapeake* left port and was intercepted and boarded by officers from the British frigate *Leopard*. Four sailors were declared to be British citizens and were removed. This incident incensed many Americans and President Jefferson and Congress quickly passed the Embargo Act of 1807, forbidding any foreign vessel to load in an American port. Coastwise, trade within America continued, but merchants had to post a bond that no trade outside of the country would occur. The Embargo Act was disastrous to American commerce and some attempted to avoid the law as represented in figure 5-3.

AMERICA BARRELS ALONG

Figure 5-3. A miller with a barrel of superfine flour is attempting to have it loaded on a foreign ship during the Embargo Act of 1807-09. Ograbme is embargo spelled backwards. In this political cartoon he is being apprehended for not having a license. From Mace, page 244.

Two years later, Congress replaced the embargo act with the Non-intercourse Act that allowed foreign trade with all countries except England and France.

After the Revolutionary War, Americans continued a migration west that persisted until the Pacific Coast was populated many years later. In 1790, the geographic center of the 3.9 million population was near the coast between Baltimore and Annapolis. Over the next one hundred years, it progressively moved west along a parallel about thirty-four miles per decade (see figure 5-4).

HISTORY OF THE BARREL IN AMERICA

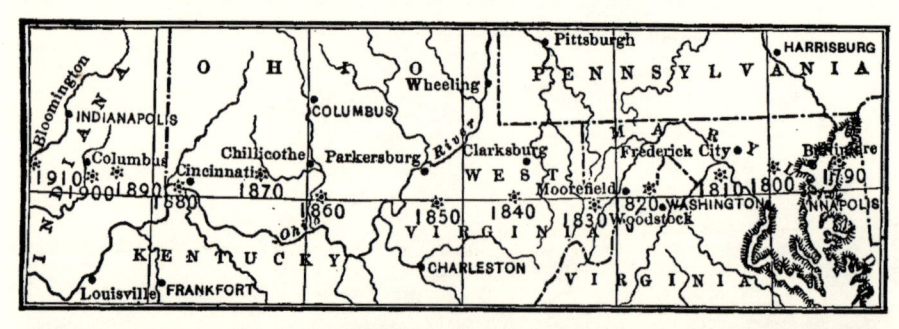

Figure 5-4. The stars or asterisks with dates identify the population center of the United States moving west along a parallel proceeding about 340 miles in 100 years. From D. H. Montgomery, *The Leading Facts of American History* (Boston: Ginn, 1917), page 180.

Sturdy Conestoga wagons provided transportation for some as the pioneers sought farmland and new opportunity. These wagons, covered with strong canvas and pulled by four to eight horses, were initially built in Pennsylvania and also hauled barrels of flour into Philadelphia as well as Baltimore, helping to grow both cities (see figure 5-5).

While figure 5-4 illustrates the specific points about which the population was uniformly distributed, it does not show how far west the pioneers had pushed the frontier line (see figure 5-6). Governmental policy and cheap land converted what was at first a trickle, into a flood, as settlers poured across the mountains.

Figure 5-5. The sturdy Conestoga wagon provided transportation for some pioneers heading west. From Allen C. Thomas, *A History of the United States* (Boston: D. C. Heath, 1901), page 259.

AMERICA BARRELS ALONG

Figure 5-6. The frontier line in 1820 is shown with an overlay of state boundaries. From S. E. Forman, *The Rise of American Commerce and Industry* (New York: Century, 1927), page 161.

In 1820, the population of the United States was 9.6 million, with a geometric center, as shown in figure 5-4, just east of Moorefield, West Virginia. Already, however, pioneers had settled as far west as Missouri and Arkansas. In their migration, it was the barrel that transported valuable food commodities such as flour, corn, sugar, fruits, and vegetables.

HISTORY OF THE BARREL IN AMERICA

A Canal and the *Constellation*

On October 26, 1825 the 340.7-mile long Erie Canal, connecting Lake Erie with the Hudson River at Waterford, New York, opened. The first fleet through, headed by the *Seneca Chief*, bore two barrels of water from Lake Erie, which were emptied by Governor DeWitt Clinton into the Atlantic Ocean celebrating "The Marriage of the Waters." The canal (see figure 5-7) facilitated America's westward migration and as noted by engineer and surveyor Roy G. Finch:

> The Erie proved to be America's greatest canal. Its effect was soon felt, not only through the state but throughout the east and Great Lakes region. Settlers flocked westward, forest gave way to sawmills and hamlets and these in turn grew into villages. Prosperous towns were established on the Great Lakes and a splendid chain of cities sprang up along the line of the Erie Canal.[1]

Figure 5-7. Erie Canal. Travel by canal boat, unlike the bumpy, dusty and noisy stagecoach, afforded the traveler a confortable and quiet ride from one location to another. The cargo, usually transported in barrels, was below deck. From Mace, page 262.

In his interesting and well-written book *USS Constellation: From Frigate to Sloop of War*, Baltimore historian Geoffrey M. Footner provides an illustration, which shows the orlop deck of the ship depicting how many barrels were arranged in the vessel's hull. A portion of the drawing, originally from the *National Archives,* is shown in figure 5-8.

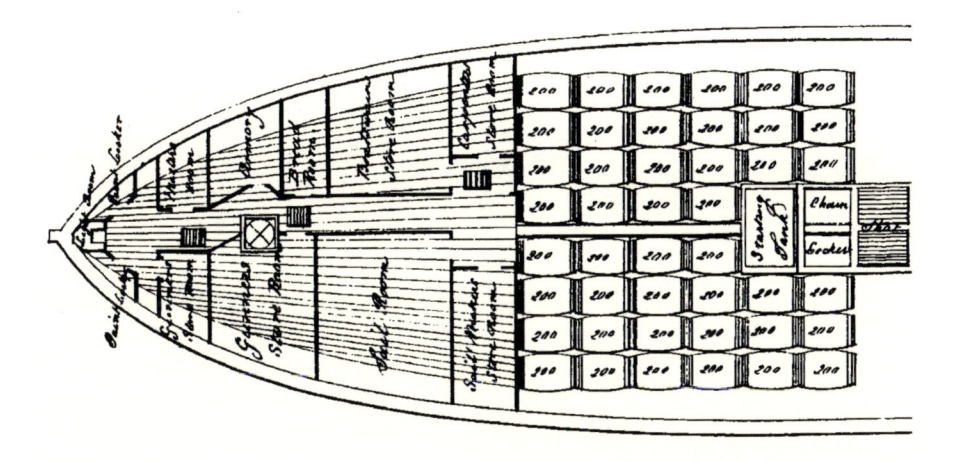

Figure 5-8. Part of the orlop deck plan of the USS *Constellation* showing the stowage of wooden barrels in the hold. From Geoffrey M. Footner, *USS Constellation: From Frigate to Sloop of War* (Annapolis: Naval Institute Press, 2003), figure 7.3.

Railroads

Other canals followed, with the Chesapeake and Delaware Canal opening in 1829. When plans were announced to construct the Chesapeake and Ohio Canal between Washington, D.C., and the Ohio River following the Potomac River westward and bypassing Baltimore, the city's leaders were alarmed. The commerce from the west flowing into the port city would be diverted; so a bold new plan was needed. This resulted in the formation of the Baltimore and Ohio Railroad, work on which started the same day as the canal in 1828, and beat the waterway to it most westward destination, Cumberland, Maryland, by eight years.

The B&O was not America's first railroad, but it did the most to establish the viability of rail service across the United States. In a couple of decades, railroads significantly overtook canals as the preferred mode for personal travel and transport of cargo, growing to ten thousand miles of track by 1850.

HISTORY OF THE BARREL IN AMERICA

Figure 5-9. Earlier than the Baltimore and Ohio Railroad, the 1831 Mohawk and Hudson Railway is shown with two barrels of wood on the tender for the steam engine's boiler. The three early passenger cars connected behind look much like stagecoaches. From Montgomery, page 224.

Oil Gushes in Pennsylvania

The most significant event that affected the American cooperage industry was the discovery of oil in Pennsylvania. The United States had grown to a population of 30.6 million in 1859 and the production of barrels for agricultural and other commodity shipping containers had increased to meet the demand. Suddenly, however, on August 27, at a depth of 69 feet on Oil Creek near Titusville, crude oil from Colonel Drake's oil well gushed to the surface (see figure 5-10). About 2,000 barrels were recovered the first year; 500,000 barrels in 1860, and ten years later the astounding volume of 5.3 million barrels. Coopers were overwhelmed in trying to meet the demand and new production techniques for barrels were urgently needed.

At this time the oil barrel (later standardized to 42 gallons)[2] was made by hand, as had been done by coopers for centuries. J.B. Wagner of Hyde Park, New York, a writer on cooperage topics, provided a description of an old cooper shop that was perhaps typical of those facilities that existed around the country:

> Anyone who has actually worked, either as a helper or a full fledged cooper in these old-time shops, and has come in contact with the peculiar, satisfying orders which circulate freely there, will never forget them. There is something indescribable about them – an inexpressible something which draws one to the place they originate. Anyone well acquainted with the scent can distinguish it readily some distance away; can follow its beckoning call easily, and sooner or later will arrive at the place from whence it came.

There is an attraction about it that pulls one like loadstone. Perhaps it comes from the woodsy smell of the freshly cut shavings on the floor of the shop; perhaps it comes from the pungent smell of the burning wood and shavings in the "cresset" in the fireplace; perhaps it comes from the warmish smell of the thoroughly heated barrel; perhaps it is all of these things combined. Whatever its source, once you have become acquainted with its combined peculiarities, it will remain as a lasting memory for a lifetime.[3]

Figure 5-10. The Pennsylvania Rock Oil Company made its first crude oil discovery, and the first in the United States, at the Drake oil well in 1859 near Titusville, Pennsylvania. From Montgomery, page 271.

About a decade before the discovery of crude oil, there began to appear machinery that performed some of the steps in the production of a barrel. The December 25, 1847 issue of *Scientific American* provided on the front page a description of an Improved Stave Jointing Machine invented by H. Law of Wilmington, North Carolina (see figure 5-11).

HISTORY OF THE BARREL IN AMERICA

Figure 5-11. Improved stave jointing machine that represented one of the first steps in automating each part of the barrel-making process. From *Scientific American*, December 25, 1874, page 105.

In a subsequent volume of *Scientific American*, a reporter had an opportunity to review Law's machine, which was installed at Burdon's Foundry at 100 Front Street in Brooklyn, New York. This report, which also mentions three previous efforts, follows:

> We visited the establishment last week and had an ocular demonstration of their performance, and we cannot but speak highly of their merits. For working sawed staves we have seen in operation the stave dressing machine of Mr. Smith of Lockport, and three years ago we saw the one belonging to Mr. Randal in Albany, and we have likewise seen the ingenious machine of Judson & Pardee, of New Haven, Conn. for split staves; but Mr. Law's is entirely different in its construction and operation from these, and it does the work handsomely, finishing 8 or 9 staves per minute. [4]

The foregoing establishes a clearer picture of some of the ongoing efforts to automate barrel making that was occurring in the late 1840s, no doubt to reduce costs and increase output. Specifically, a mention is made of sawed staves, an invention generally credited to Baxter D. Whitney who developed the cylinder stave-sawing machine around 1850.[5]

In 1851, E.G. Brown of Montville, Maine, invented and produced a barrelhead-making machine. The head was clamped into a hand-operated turntable, which moved the edge of the head through a

AMERICA BARRELS ALONG

set of power-driven rotating cutters to produce the desire angles on each side (see figure 5-12).

About 1854, John Benson introduced a stave bucker that had two curved stationary knives set about three quarters of an inch apart. A rough stave or blank was forced though, producing both the inside and outside curvature on the "bucked" stave.[6] This eliminated much work, since the cooper no longer had to fashion the stave at the block with drawknives (see figure 5-13). This invention, along with the cylinder saw and head cutter, represented noteworthy steps in automating the production of a barrel, but machines to list and join the stave, truss the barrel, cut the howel, chime and croze, and integrate these into a production line were years away.

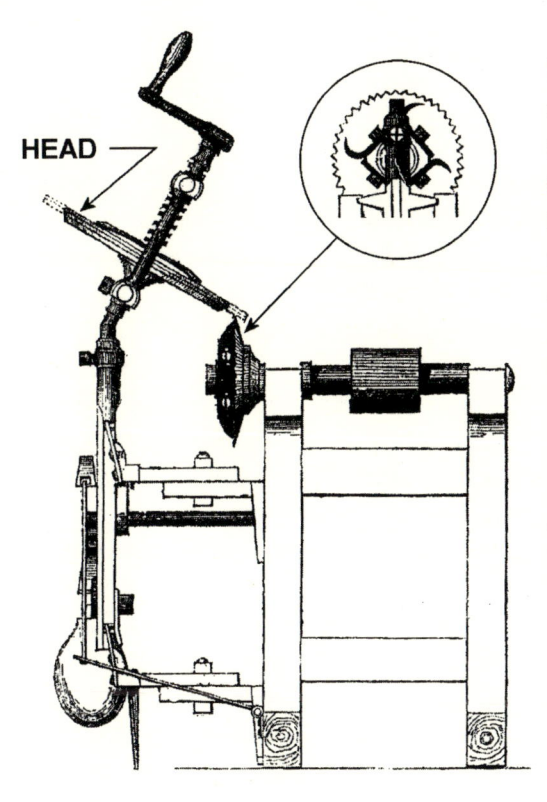

Figure 5-12. Head-making machine. The head is mounted on a turntable, which can be rotated by the handle. The combination dish-saw and datto head are driven by a flat belt to the pulley. Shown in the circle (above right) is the view of the cutting heads as seen from the left side. Adapted by the author from the E.G. Brown 1851 catalog as found in Kenneth Cope, *American Cooperage Machinery and Tools*, page 19.

HISTORY OF THE BARREL IN AMERICA

Figure 5-13. John Benson's steam-powered dresser or "bucker" that used knives to produce staves with curved sides. From Coyne, *Cooperage Industry*, page 23.

Civil War Intervenes

The War of Southern Succession was largely economically based on the somewhat misguided belief that federal tariffs placed an unfair governmental cost on the agrarian South to the benefit of the more industrialized North. This was further aggravated in that the South was always cash-poor and depended on northern-based banks for capital to fund their ever-expanding agricultural growth of king cotton, tobacco, sugar, indigo, and rice. Because of this, crops grown in the South were often shipped to New York City on Northern-owned vessels and exported to foreign ports where imports were loaded and transported back to the South for sale. The middlemen and northern shipping interest benefited from this. The triangular trade seemed an advantage to the North and led to the belief that Southern political independence was the answer for its capital-poor economy.

As England and France benefited greatly from the South's cotton, some Southern political leaders believed that support from these countries would be forthcoming in their struggle for independence – which was rationalized to be somewhat akin to the independence won by America in the Revolutionary War. In the end, however, this was not the case. England, in particular, found that, on balance, trade with the North was more economically beneficial – receiving barrels of wheat rather then bales of cotton in exchange for manufactured goods, particularly arms.

After Virginia seceded from the Union, Confederate troops were directly across the Potomac River from Washington D.C., so President Lincoln ordered federal troops to protect the city. This also required the army be fed, so barrels of flour were stored in the basement of the Senate Chamber for use by the government bakery under the Capitol (see figure 5-14).

Figure 5-14. Barrels of flour are shown being rolled into the Capitol for use by the onsite federal bakery. From Stanley Kimmel, *Mr. Lincoln's Washington* (New York: Coward-McCain, 1957), page 49.

Another problem soon manifested itself, as soldiers with idle time were apt to frequent local taverns and inns and consume an inappropriate amount of alcohol. Military retaliation soon followed as one newspaper reported, "The provost guard visited the barroom of Mr. Kernan and nine barrels of whiskey were poured upon the ground."[7] This led to signs refusing to sell alcohol to soldiers by bar owners who did not want to see "profits poured down the drain." See figure 5-15.

Figure 5-15. Military authorities empty a barrel of whiskey belonging to an inn owner who had sold alcohol to soldiers. From Kimmel, page 89.

AMERICA BARRELS ALONG

During the war it was reported, "Lincoln's prospects for re-election in 1864 seemed so remote that he once publicly promised to 'cooperate with the president-elect.'"[8] He won easily prompting the political cartoon shown in figure 5-16.

Figure 5-16. Long Abraham. Lincoln was perceived a little taller after his re-election in November 1864. From Kimmel, page 154.

President Lincoln had a very difficult time finding generals the caliber of Robert E. Lee and finally selected Ulysses S. Grant as his commander. Others close to the president were not so taken with his choice and reported to Lincoln that Grant was prone to drink too much. "Tell me what brand of whiskey Grant drinks," Lincoln was reported to have said, "I would like to send a barrel of it to my other generals."[9]

The bloody war came to an end on April 9, 1865 when Robert E. Lee surrendered his entire army at Appomattox Court House, Virginia. The Union had been preserved, but it would be decades before the South recovered.

Barrel Machinery Improves

Two brothers, Edward and Britain Holmes, founded E. & B. Holmes in 1859 to produce machinery for making barrels. By 1874, they had developed a complete line of equipment that was installed in a barrel factory operated by sugar refiners Havemeyer & Elder in Brooklyn, New York. A reporter from *Scientific American* visited the factory for a few hours and filed this report:

> We cannot describe the noise which saluted us as deafening, for the word fails to express it; it was equal to that of a regiment of boilers riveters, and worse than a few dozen steam hammers, so that remarks of an explanatory nature were out of the question, or else imparted by the aid of pantomime. Picking our way between belts, and dodging the barrels wich [*sic*] were constantly flying about the room, we reached a space where loose staves were heaped, and where the workmen were busily at work setting up the barrels before delivering them to the machinery. The setting up form is composed of two heavy circles of iron, secured together and bolted to the floor; from these rise short standards which support a hoop. The staves are set in between the iron circles, and fitted carefully together. The iron truss hooks [hoops], which were previously placed in proper position, are lifted up by hand so as to embrace the lower portion of the staves and hold them in place, when the whole is lifted out of the frame. One half of the barrel is now tightly held together, but the remainder was still open and flaring. To secure this in similar manner, a rope was passed around the flaring ends and taken to a hand windlass, a few turns of which brought the staves together, when the truss hoops were slipped over the extremities, and the barrel was ready to be heated in order to cause its staves to assume the curved shape.[10]

Although not illustrated in the article, a hand-operated windlass is shown in the E. & B. Holmes catalog that has been reproduced in the book, *American Cooperage Machinery and Tools* (see figure 5-17).

Figure 5-17. Hand operated windlass used to draw staves together to install trussing hoops. From Cope, page 62.

Thereafter the barrel is placed over a heater "being closed with a sheet of iron cover, which was let down from above." After the wood had been thoroughly warmed, and the staves took the set of the shape of the barrel, it was necessary to level the container, "its object is to bring the cask into a shape that, when on end, it will stand perpendicular and not lean in any direction."[11] The leveling device is shown in figure 5-18.

Figure 5-18. Barrel leveler. From *Scientific American*, March 28, 1897, page 194.

The barrel was rolled across the floor to the trussing machine, where it was put into "the clutches of a number of hooked bars which protruded up through the floor, as seen in figure 5-19. The article in *Scientific American* provided a description: "The machine, we noted, was operated by a single man and with great ease. A strong power was brought to bear on each hoop, which thoroughly trussed the barrel with remarkable rapidity."[12]

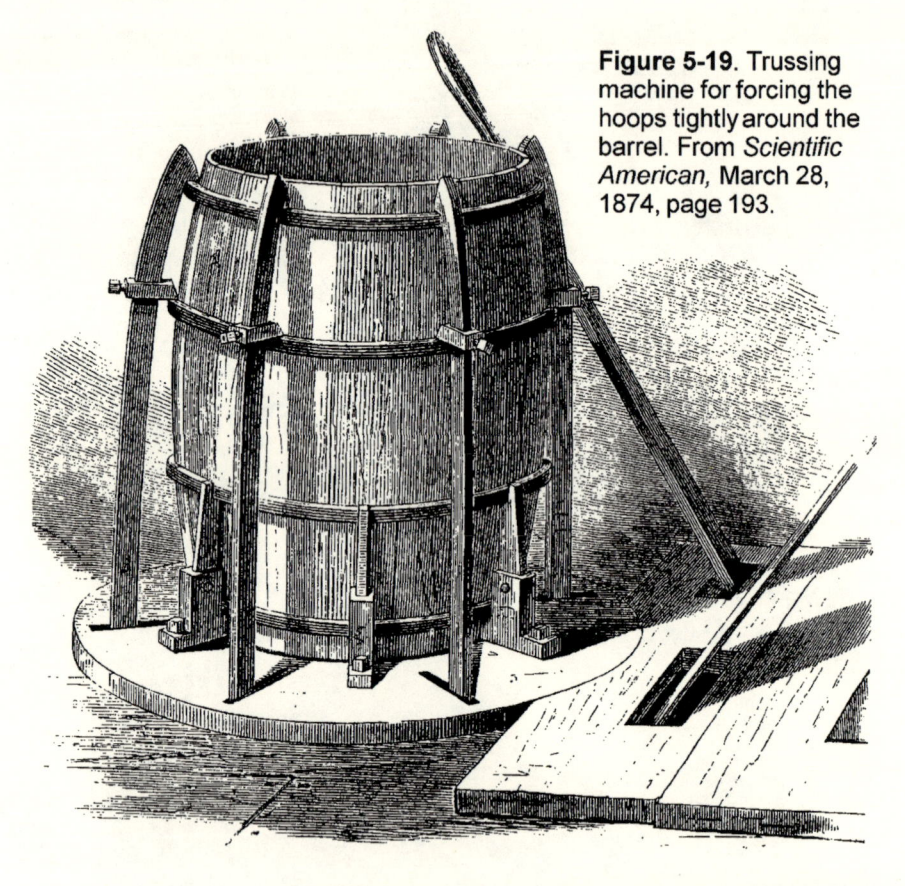

Figure 5-19. Trussing machine for forcing the hoops tightly around the barrel. From *Scientific American,* March 28, 1874, page 193.

The next operation of chamfering and crozing was described in the magazine as "a machine which is unquestionably an invention of extraordinary merit and ingenuity." The article goes on to state "Some idea of the efficacy of the machine . . . will therefore be formed when we state that it chamfers, howels, levels, and crozes a cask of imperfect periphery with the same exactness as if it were a perfect circle, finishes both ends at once, and runs of from 800 to 1,200 barrels per day with ease."[13] See figure 5-20.

Figure 5-20. The Holmes' chamfering and crozing machine, which accomplish what some coopers thought was impossible. It automatically chamfered, howeled and crozed both ends of a barrel in one operation. From *Scientific American*, March 28, 1874, page 193.

The remaining steps of boring the bung and installing the heads were accomplished by hand, but it is clear most of the critical operations heretofore accomplished by a cooper can now be done by machinery. A storeroom at the facility contained a reported 25,000 barrels. The small barrel shop had been transformed into a huge barrel factory and no longer was the cooper in command of his future. In fact, the word cooper was slowly disappearing from the language, being replaced by "hooper" or "hooper-cooper," an insult to his rapidly automated trade.[14]

The Cooper Fights Back

The barrel-making equipment threatened many centuries of an established lifestyle enjoyed by the cooper and was very much resented. There were threats of destroying machinery as it was

HISTORY OF THE BARREL IN AMERICA

installed, but mechanization moved forward without incident. *Scientific American* in 1874 reported, "not long since, strikes of considerable magnitude occurred among the coopers of the State [New York]. These movements owed their origin, among other causes, to the introduction into the market and use, by the barrel manufacturers, of improved machinery by means of which labor of skilled mechanics was, in a large measure, dispensed with, and the work readily accomplished by ordinary day laborers." [15]

Such attempts to thwart the progress of producing better quality barrels at a lower cost did not succeed. In a competitive market, every producer constantly strives to outdistance his competition by substituting machinery for labor where there are resulting cost benefits to the manufacturer and, ultimately, the consumer. For the cooper, however, this was not desirable progress; the small cooperages shops (see figure 5-21) were part of a long tradition and evoked fond memories.

Regarding "The Old Hand Cooper" of the mid-1870s, Coyne noted his "obstinate and carefree manner no doubt had a great deal to do with the initial introduction of machinery." He perceptively writes:

> Usually Saturday of each week was pay day, and of course the temptation to lounge around the shop and chat with one another was most often too great to be overcome by the average cooper, so that day was considered lost so far as production in barrel making was concerned. Furthermore, the old-time cooper had the reputation of being a strong and lusty beer drinker, and naturally he couldn't afford to let that reputation lapse.
>
> So early on Saturday morning the big brewery wagon would drive up to the shop. Several coopers would club together, each paying his proper share, and one of them would call out of the window to the driver, "Bring me a 'Goose Egg,'" meaning a half barrel of beer. Then others would buy "Goose Eggs" and there would be a merry time all around. . . . Little groups of jolly fellows would often sit around an upright turned barrel playing poker, using rivets for chips, until they had received their pay and the "Goose Egg" was dry. . . .
>
> Many cooper used to spend [Sunday] sharpening up their tools, carrying in stock, discussing current events and getting things in shape for the big day of work on the morrow. Thus, "Blue Monday" was something of a tradition with the coopers, and the day was also more or less lost as far as production was concerned.

"Can't do much today, but I'll give her hell tomorrow" appeared to be the Monday slogan. But bright and early Tuesday morning "Give her hell" they would, banging away lustily for the rest of the week until Saturday, which was pay day again, and its thoughts of the "Goose Eggs."[16]

Figure 5-21. Shown is the old plant of K. W. Jacobs Cooperage Company in the city famous for beer, Milwaukee, Wisconsin. From Coyne, page 71.

Such was one week in the life of the cooper during the mid-1870s, but with the introduction of barrel-making machinery, this vignette rapidly faded from the landscape.

Flour Barrels

Wheat flour provided a substantial amount of work for the cooperage industry, as can be seen the table 5-1. In 1860, flour barrels holding 196 pounds numbered 39.8 million, growing to 105.8 million by 1900.

HISTORY OF THE BARREL IN AMERICA

Table 5-1. Shown is the production of flour, beer, and whiskey in the United States (1860-1940). From U.S. census records except where noted.

Year	Barrel of Flour (Million)	Barrels of Beer (Million)	Barrels of Whiskey (Million)
1860	39.8	-	-
1870	47.9	6.6	1.5
1880	64.3	13.3	1.9
1890	83.3	27.6	2.3
1900	105.8	39.5	2.2
1910	107.2	59.5	1.7[17]
1920	130.4	9.2	-
1930	123.6[18]	3.7	-
1940	110.9	54.9	1.9

Around this time cotton and paper bags[19] were becoming available and some buyers preferred flour sacks, since they were easier to handle than wooden barrels. Because flour completion was very keen, the buyer's wishes were adopted, thereby decreasing the work for the barrel industry.

Coopers, however, fought back and in 1901 and placed an ad in the trade publication *Barrel and Box* instigating a movement to buy flour in barrels (see figure 5-22). Table 5-1 shows a continued growth in the production of flour, which was still measured in barrels, but the sacks gradually took over, and even today paper bags remain the container of choice for flour at the grocery store.

Figure 5-22. As the flour industry switched to cotton and paper sacks, coopers encouraged their co-workers to stay with the traditional barrel, Barrel from Coyne, page 36; sack from Hal Morgan, *Symbols of America* (New York: Viking, 1986), page 122.

Beer Barrels

Like flour, there was also a tremendous growth in the production of beer in the United States, but unlike the generally discarded flour barrel,[20] the 36-gallon beer container could be reused many times.[21] As production grew, new containers were required and a percentage of the old containers needed replacement. So the industry, at least for a while, provided coopers steady work.

For the decade of 1920 and early into the 1930s, prohibition was in effect and beer quantities dropped dramatically, no doubt limited to the export market. By 1940, however, it rose almost to the 1910 level, but with this rapid increase, the coopers could not meet the demand and steel barrels were introduced. These durable containers eventually replaced the wooden barrels.

It is interesting to examine the distribution of beer production in the United States in 1880. An illustration shows this in figure 5-23. The total for all states is 14.9 million barrels, which is slightly higher than the 13.3 million in table 5-1 derived from U.S. census data.

HISTORY OF THE BARREL IN AMERICA

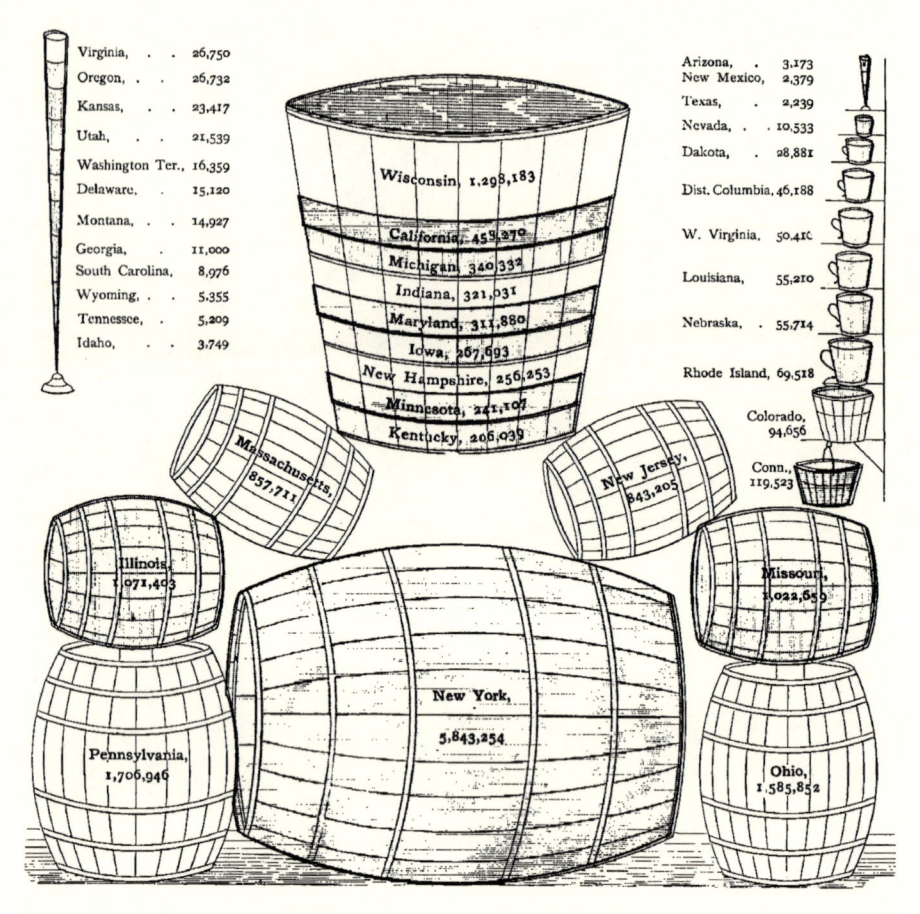

Virginia,	26,750
Oregon,	26,732
Kansas,	23,417
Utah,	21,539
Washington Ter.,	16,359
Delaware,	15,120
Montana,	14,927
Georgia,	11,000
South Carolina,	8,976
Wyoming,	5,355
Tennessee,	5,209
Idaho,	3,749

Wisconsin, 1,298,183
California, 453,270
Michigan, 340,332
Indiana, 321,031
Maryland, 311,880
Iowa, 267,693
New Hampshire, 256,253
Minnesota, 241,107
Kentucky, 206,039

Arizona,	3,173
New Mexico,	2,379
Texas,	2,239
Nevada,	10,533
Dakota,	28,881
Dist. Columbia,	46,188
W. Virginia,	50,410
Louisiana,	55,210
Nebraska,	55,714
Rhode Island,	69,518
Colorado,	94,656
Conn.,	119,523

Massachusetts, 857,711
New Jersey, 843,205
Illinois, 971,403
Missouri, 1,022,559
Pennsylvania, 1,706,946
New York, 5,843,254
Ohio, 1,585,852

Figure 5-23. Beer production in the United States in 1880 is shown by state. From R. S. Peale, *Peale's Popular Educator and Cyclopedia of Reference* (Baltimore: Hill and Harvey Publisher, 1885), page 575.

Whiskey Barrels

It has been reported that "By the early 1780s settlers in Kentucky and Tennessee were taking whiskey down the Ohio and Tennessee Rivers to the Mississippi and then down to New Orleans – a trip which lasted as long as three months. Records for 1810 indicate Kentucky, Tennessee, Virginia, North Carolina, Ohio, and Pennsylvania produced *millions* of gallons of whiskey."[22] Corn was the main ingredient and sold for about 50 cents per bushel, but a bushel could yield three to five gallons of whiskey worth perhaps $2 per gallon. As whiskey did not spoil, it could be kept for some time before a quantity was accumulated and the down-river trek was made.

The whiskey was transported in barrels that had been slightly charred by the cooper on the inside as a result of heating so the staves could be formed into the desired barrel shape. After reaching New Orleans, the whiskey was then shipped to an East Coast market. Storage by the maker plus shipping delays sometimes resulted in a time between distillation and consumption as much as one year or more.

During this time the whiskey aged, taking on a slight red color, and becoming mellower, hence creating a more favorable market demand compared to whiskey that had been recently distilled. Soon the makers experimented with charring the barrels beyond what had been done incidentally by the coopers. Aged whiskey was born – eventually making the states of Kentucky and Tennessee synonymous with a quality product.

For more than one and one-half centuries (1607-1862), except for the years between 1791 and 1802 and 1812 and 1815, making whiskey in America without a license was legal. The activity was inevitably linked to freedom, and taxes thereupon were often bitterly resented by back-country pioneers, particularly in the South. After the Civil War, however, a cash-strapped federal government started enforcing the tax on distilled spirits.

Using the number of gallons taxed, starting in 1870, along with an average of 48 gallons per container, the number of barrels can be determined, as shown in table 5-1. No legal distilled spirits were produced during Prohibition, which includes the years 1920 and 1930. Compared to flour and beer barrels, the number is insignificant, but since whiskey, along with wine, is still aged in charred white oak barrels, this remains today one of the last bastions for the cooperage industry (see figure 5-24).

HISTORY OF THE BARREL IN AMERICA

Figure 5-24. Shown is a stack of barrels of distilled liquors used in an advertisement of a Baltimore distributor, W. T. Walters & Company. From George W. Howard, *The Monumental City its Past History and Present Resources* (Baltimore: J. D. Ehlers, 1873), page 127.

Government Standardization

Sizes of barrels had principally remained the purview of the various states until 1912 when the federal government defined the size and volume of the "dry capacity" barrel. A volume of 7,056 cubic inches or 104 dry quarts was required with a tolerance described "as nearly as possible." Specifically, apple barrels with other capacities were to be so marked. In 1915, the law was changed, requiring all dry goods except cranberries to have the same dimensions as the dry capacity barrel, but now specifying the stave thickness to be a quarter inch. With this new law, apple barrels not meeting the 7,056 cubic inch capacity were not legal for U.S. trade.

In addition, the 1915 law provided for a standard barrel for fruits or other dry commodities, besides cranberries, which was the same as the dry good barrel except the stave thickness was specified to be 0.4 inches. The dimensions of a cranberry barrel were also specified; all of these are summarized in Table 5-2.[23]

Table 5-2. Size and capacity of barrels defined by the U.S. government in 1912 and 1915. All dimension in inches.

	1912 Dry Capacity Barrel	1915 All Dry Goods Barrel	1915 Fruits & Dry Commodities Barrel	1915 Cran-berries Barrel
Stave Length	28-1/2	28-1/2	28-1/2	28-1/2
Stave Thickness	-	1/4	0.4	0.4
Head Diameter	17-1/8	17-1/8	17-1/8	16-1/4
Head-to-Head Spacing	26	26	26	25-1/4
Circumference Outside of Bilge	64	64	64	58-1/2
Capacity (cu. in.)	7056[a]	7056[b]	7056[c]	-

The King of Packages

Coyne writes, "With the turn of the twentieth century the cooperage industry 'became of age,' so to speak, for it was then that the trade entered into the days of it greatest scope and productivity. The wooden barrel was almost universally used as a shipping container of bulk commodities and it became known as the king of packages."[24]

According to Coyne, there were 408 active establishments in the tight barrels and headings division of the cooperage industry in 1908. The output of slack barrels and kegs, along with the country's population from 1906 to 1910, is shown in table 5-3. In 1909, more

---
[a] Smaller apple barrels were to be marked in one-inch gothic letters with fractional amounts.
[b] One-third, one-half and three-quarter barrels became illegal for domestic trade.
[c] Other forms allowed if capacity is met.

slack containers were produced than there were people living the United States. With such a proliferation of barrels, it is easy to understand how the packages were considered so ordinary they were not considered worthy of discussion, hence seldom mentioned in historical writing.[25]

Table 5-3. Slack barrels and kegs produced from 1906 to 1910. Barrel data is from Coyne, page 39, and population data from U.S. census.

Year	U.S. Population (Million)	Barrels Produced (Million)
1906	85	68
1907	87	74
1908	89	97
1909	90	127
1910	92	91

The decades of 1900, 1910 and 1920 were the heydays of the cooperage industry, but on the horizon was competition from "steel, corrugated paper, fiberboard, and even aluminum"[26] packages that were lighter in weight and could be shipped with better *volumetric efficiency* compared to the barrel.[27] The 55-gallon steel drum, often incorrectly called a barrel, became a major competitor of wooden containers because of its robustness and reusability.

Many item previously shipped in bulk, such as pickles, vinegar, and crackers, were starting to be broken down into tin cans, bottles, and cellophane-wrapped cardboard packages that could be sold directly to the consumer without having to be individually weighed. The old country store (see figure 5-25), with barrels of goods setting about, would eventually transition to the mom and pop grocery store, then the regional grocery store, and finally today to the centrally-owned supermarkets chain stores.

AMERICA BARRELS ALONG

Figure 5-25. Country store is depicted with the owner weighing out several pounds of flour, and the assistant weighing the whole of the young lady and part of the dog. From Emerson E. White, *First Book of Arithmetic* (New York: American Book, 1890), page 147.

Barrels Contained Everything

While wooden barrels gradually gave way to other types of packages, their importance is obvious through their images in business letterheads and invoices. A Baltimore merchant displayed the barrel on a January 19, 1924 bill sent to a client, which is shown in figure 5-26.

Figure 5-26. Shown is an Image from the top of an invoice from Bronner, Marvel & Headley, general commission merchants in Baltimore. From an invoice in the author's collection.

HISTORY OF THE BARREL IN AMERICA

A catalog of *Home-Trade* advertised paint sold by the barrel, shown in figure 5-27.

Figure 5-27. Black paint sold by the barrel is advertised in the *Home-Trade*r catalog of circa 1914.

A Valley Oil Company letterhead used the three barrels shown in figure 5-28 depicting lard, steam cylinder oil, and engine and machine oil.

Figure 5-28. Three barrels shown on the 1915 letterhead of the Valley Oil Company. From a letterhead in the author's collection

Not an everyday product for most consumers, an eagle is shown in figure 5-29, proudly holding a small barrel or keg of embalming fluid.

AMERICA BARRELS ALONG

Figure 5-29. Imperial brand embalming fluid advertisement of 1898 combines the robustness of a barrel and the strength of an eagle. From Morgan, *Symbols of America*, page 19.

Figure 5-30. Making ale at P. Ballantine & Son's Brewery in Newark, New Jersey. From *Scientific American*, March 15, 1879, page 159.

These images provide a sampling of some of the hundreds of items shipped in barrels. Many more are listed in Appendix A. In addition, Chapter 9 addresses how the ubiquitous container found it way into the American language.

HISTORY OF THE BARREL IN AMERICA

[1] Roy G. Finch, *The Story of the New York State Canals* (1925; reprint, Unknown: State of New York, 1998), p. 7.
[2] For an excellent discussion of how the oil barrel became 42 gallons, see Robert E. Hardwicke, *The Oilman's Barrel* (Norman OK, University of Oklahoma Press, 1958).
[3] As quoted in Franklin E. Coyne, *The Development of the Cooperage Industry in the United States* (Chicago: Lumbers Buyers Publishing, 1940), p. 18.
[4] *Scientific American*, December 9, 1848, p. 93.
[5] Kenneth L. Cope, *American Cooperage Machinery and Tools* (Mendham, NJ: Astragal Press, 2003), p. 199.
[6] Coyne, p. 16.
[7] Stanley Kimmel, *Mr. Lincoln's Washington* (New York: Coward-McCain, 1957), p. 98.
[8] Editors of Year, *Pictorial History of America* (Los Angeles, CA: Year), p. 204.
[9] *The Columbia World of Quotations*, 1996, as found at www.bartleby.com, July 3, 2004, with search for "barrel."
[10] *Scientific American*, March 28, 1874, p. 193.
[11] Ibid.
[12] Ibid.
[13] Ibid., p.194.
[14] Coyne, p. 24.
[15] Ibid., p. 22.
[16] Ibid., p. 21.
[17] The 1910 and 1940 (actually 1939) data are from Coyne, pp. 45–46.
[18] For flour, the 1930 datum is actually from 1929.
[19] The first paper bag or "poke" was patented May 28, 1867. See Eric Sloane, *The Cracker Barrel* (New York: Funk & Wagnalls, 1967), p. 93.
[20] Sometimes bakers would pack hardtack or biscuits in empty flour barrels for shipment.
[21] Robert E. Hardwick, p. 43. Today a barrel of beer contains 31 gallons. See www.sfbrewing.com/ask, Dec. 25, 2004.
[22] Mark H. Waymack and James F. Harris, *Classic American Whiskeys* (Chicago: Open Court, 1995), p. 9.
[23] See www.sizes.com/units/barrelUSdry_goods.htm, Aug. 30, 2004, for the information source used in this section.
[24] Coyne, p. 33.
[25] Except for books and articles dealing with cooperage and books of quotations, the author has seldom been able to find "barrel" listed in the index of a book or a periodical.
[26] Coyne, p. 65.
[27] Volumetric efficiency is concerned with having package shapes that will efficiently stack together to maximize the amount of product in a given shipping container, say a boxcar.

Chapter 6
Those Inventive Americans

For transporting American products such as flour, sugar, apples, and crackers from one location to another, the barrel performed superbly. Once the container arrived at its destination, say a general store in the country, the head was removed so customers could purchase its contents in small quantities. To keep insects and rodents out, it was necessary to replace the head, or in some way cover the top of the barrel. It was perhaps inevitable that enterprising merchants would find solutions to this problem, such as the one invented by G.W. Lindsey of Fredericksburg, Virginia and published in *Scientific American* (see figure 6-1).[1]

Accessible Heads

Figure 6-1. Barrel cover that can be applied after the head is removed. The cover is positioned on the top of the barrel and kept in place by clips and U-shaped wires driven into the staves. A handle on top allows a hinged lid to be opened to access contents. From *Scientific American,* May 25, 1889, page 323.

HISTORY OF THE BARREL IN AMERICA

W. Wirt Hodsden of Smithfield, Virginia, invented a simple but effective barrel cover that could easily be changed from one barrel to another as the container's contents were sold. It is shown in figure 6-2.

Figure 6-2 Barrel cover with rotating lid. The bottom portion of the cover is slightly wider than one-half of the barrel's diameter and is encompassed with a hoop, which fits sugly over the top of the barrel. There is a wooden pin through both the top and bottom portions that allows the top to be rotated to open and close the access. From *Scientific American*, October 30, 1886, page 274.

The two preceding examples represent covers that could be applied by the user after the barrelhead had been removed. In other instances, however, an inventor focused on changing the basic design of the head that would be installed when the barrel was manufactured. One such design patented by Alexander Hanvey of Steubenville, Ohio, is shown in figure 6-3.

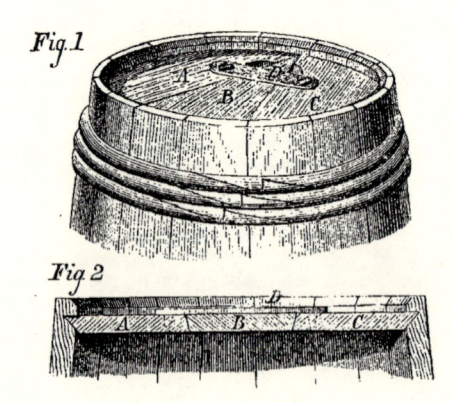

Figure 6-3. Removable barrel head. In Fig. 1 clip D, secured by two screws, is removed allowing the V-shaped headpiece B to be lifted upwards from the pointed end. In Fig. 2, it can be seen the edges of B are tapered so there is no interference with A and C as this is done. From *Scientific American*, February 7, 1874, page 86.

This approach had the added advantage it could be used to reseal the head of the barrel if it were later filled with a product to be shipped to another location.

Francisco J. Oliver of Brooklyn, New York, invented the improved head shown in figure 6-4. This design required a special croze in the barrel staves.

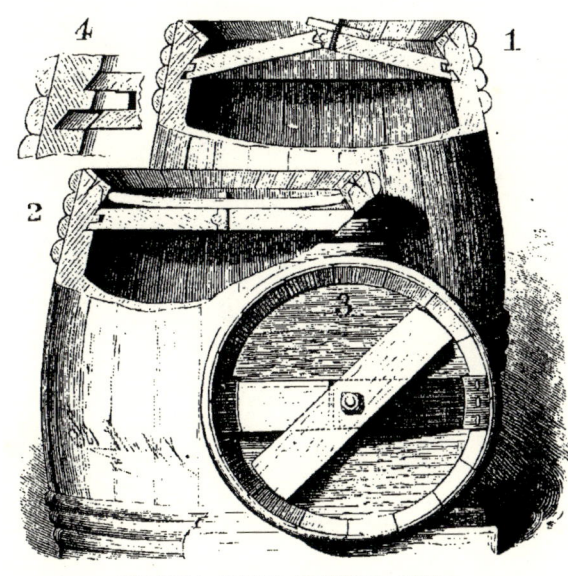

Figure 6-4. Three-piece removable head. The head is inserted as shown in Fig. 1, and the locking bar is rotated 90 degrees as illustrated in fig. 2. Fig. 3 shows how the bar is turned about the center bolt. From *Scientific American*, April 10, 1886, page 226.

OLIVER'S NOVEL BARREL HEAD.

Some products shipped in a barrel, such as herring, pork, and pickles, were submerged in a solution of salty water to keep them fresh during transit. Once the merchant removed the head there was a tendency for the contents to float above the brine's surface, leading to spoilage. It also attracted flying and crawling insects. Inserting a circular disk slightly smaller than the head into the barrel and weighting it down with a brick or stone corrected this problem. To access the contents, the weight would be removed with one hand, whereupon the thumb and forefinger of the other hand would be inserted into holes in the disk and it would be lifted out of the barrel. After the product had been removed, the merchant used a complementary two-handed procedure to replace the disk and weight.

HISTORY OF THE BARREL IN AMERICA

John J. Friederichs and Henry C. Fliege of Calumet, Michigan, patented a better idea, which could be operated with one hand that could be kept dry. It is shown in figure 6-5.

Figure 6-5. Inside barrel cover. This device is wedged between opposite sides of the barrel. Different size containers can be accomodated by adjusting the clip held by the wing nut. From *Scientific American*, September 23, 1893, page 197.

Moving Barrels

Another difficulty facing the merchant was moving barrels from one location to another. The barrel was its own wheel and on level or reasonably inclined smooth grades, it could be rolled. But going from the ground into the back of a wagon, or up the steps to a store required the container be lifted. Its shape did easily facilitate this. William Brown of Greenpoint, New York, invented a clever device that temporarily provided side handles for a barrel. It is shown in figure 6-6.

Figure 6-6. Barrel lifting device. The metal strap on the bottom of the side handles is adjustable to fit different diameter barrels. The top of the handles are sharp enough to dig into the sides of the barrel to secure them in place. From *Scientific American*, November 22, 1879, page 327.

Another way to move barrels and also provide a fixture for dispensing oils and other liquids was patented by James H. Stansbury and Isaac U. Hyatt, the latter of Jamaica, New York. It is shown in figure 6-7.

Figure 6-7. Barrel Truck. Starting in an upright position, the bottom lip of the truck was pushed under the edge of a barrel and the support adjusted to be flush with the top of the container. The truck was tilted horizonally and rolled to the desired location and rested on the handles. From *Scientific American*, March 15, 1890, page 165.

HISTORY OF THE BARREL IN AMERICA

Once small barrels or kegs were emptied, their usefulness was limited since it was not convenient to carry them from one place to another. John H. Scheel of New York City invented a carrying handle that was easily applied, converting the containers into a bucket or pail.[2] The device is shown in figure 6-8.

Figure 6-8. Convertable keg. By removing the top chime hoop and installing a new hoop with a built-in bail, it was possible to transform kegs and small barrels into easily carried buckets or pails. From *Scientific American*, April 17, 1886, page 242.

Butter Churns

The task of milking a cow usually fell to one of the young girls in the family. She generally sat on a three-legged stool, but may have used the combination device shown in figure 6-9.

Figure 6-9. Milking stool with built-in bucket holder. From *Scientific American*, January 29, 1881, page 67.

THOSE INVENTIVE AMERICANS

During the eighteenth and early nineteenth centuries, most households had a cow and a butter churn of some sort. Churns came in a large variety of sizes, shapes and designs – each touted as being better or improved over the competition. John T. Mark of Strawn, Kansas, patented "an improved churn" shown in figure 6-10, in which a small barrel was rotated by a handle. As it was unlikely the barrel was completely full of liquid, the contents would have sloshed about, making the turning force very uneven, hence difficult to use.

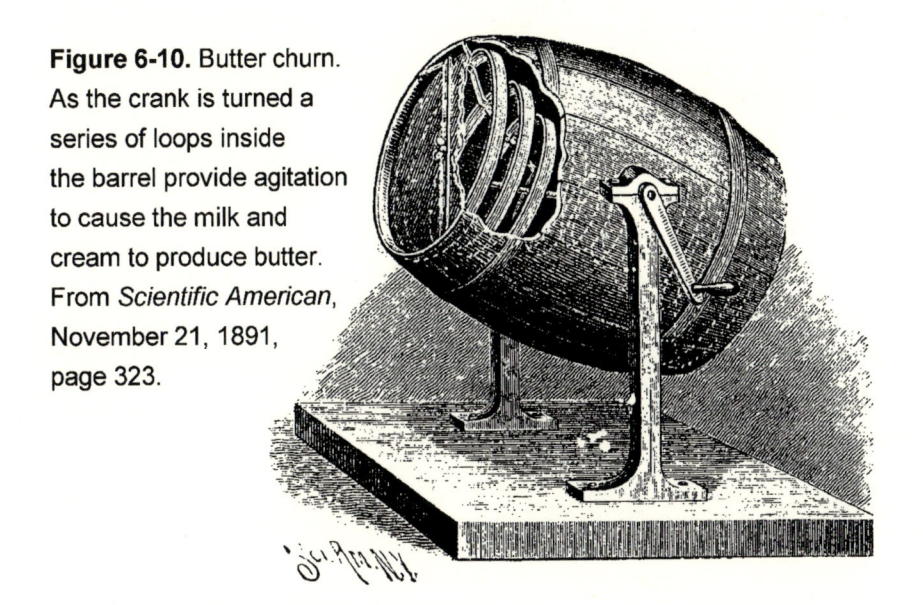

Figure 6-10. Butter churn. As the crank is turned a series of loops inside the barrel provide agitation to cause the milk and cream to produce butter. From *Scientific American*, November 21, 1891, page 323.

A churn that was much easier to turn can be seen in figure 6-11. Patented by Henry Hays of Bridgeport, California, the barrel remains stationary while the handle turned an inside paddle. This type of design is far larger than would have been required in most households, and may have found application in a commercial establishment. The inventor was so enthralled with the operation of the churn, he suggested, "A washing machine can be constructed according to the same principle."[3]

Figure 6-11. Barrel remains fixed on the support and the handle turns an inside paddle, not seen. From *Scientific American*, November 10, 1883, page 290.

A smaller and more practical butter churn, invented by E.W. Shepherd of Wilmington, Ohio, that would have likely found use in a domestic application, is shown in figure 6-12. Gearing provided a dasher speed faster than the rotation of the handle. The dasher revolved on an "antifriction socket" on the bottom of the churn.

Figure 6-12. Butter churn for domestic use. Note the inside protruding cross-section of each stave, which casues the cream to be "thrown into violent agitation." From *Scientific American*, May 13, 1876, page 310.

THOSE INVENTIVE AMERICANS

Cooling Beer

If a barrel of beer were to be enjoyed, most drinkers preferred it to be cooled. John Hoffman of Toledo, Ohio, invented a way to install a metal cooling tube in barrels, shown in figure 6-13.

Figure 6-13. Cooling beer. A metal tube is inserted between the heads, which can accept ice for cooling the contents. From *Scientific American,* September 15, 1877, page 166.

John Hoerr of Denison, Texas, invented a galvanized or enameled insert for a barrel that could be charged with a mixture of ice and salt to keep beer cool (see figure 6-14).

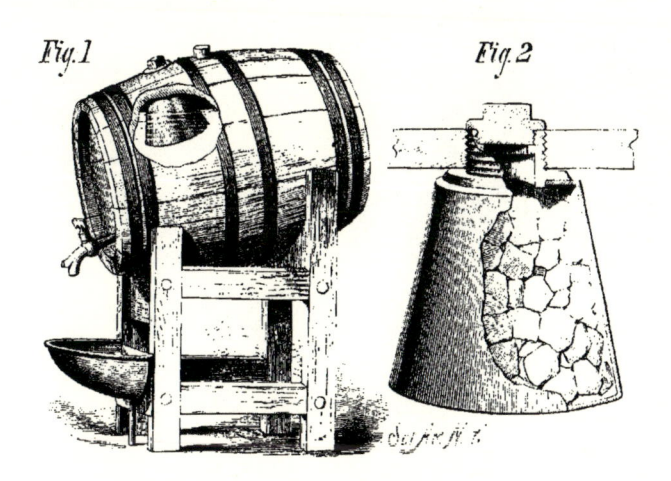

Figure 6-14. Cooling beer using an internal tank. Fig. 1 shows a cutaway of the beer barrel with the cooling tank installed. Fig. 2 depicts the tank filled with ice and salt. Using this procedure it was possible, according to the inventor, to keep beer cool for "a considerable length of time."

HISTORY OF THE BARREL IN AMERICA

Special Barrels

Inventive Americans were always coming up with ways to improve the container that was used to ship hundreds of different products. One such touted "improvement" was not actually an improvement, but an entirely new design made to look like the familiar barrel. By emulating the traditional barrel shape, the new configuration would draw attention, but its use raised some questions about its replacement of the robust cask. Invented by J.W. Adams of Laurel, Delaware, the vented lattice-type barrel is shown below in figure 6-15.

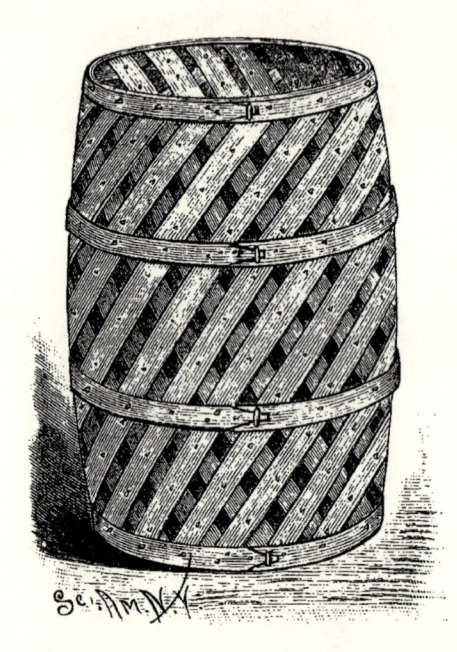

Figure 6-15. Improved barrel. This design is actually closer to a large basket than the traditional barrel. It is described as "two or more layers of splints" being nailed to each other. The construction posed difficulties in that exposed nail points would have been troublesome. Also the attachment of the heads in the description was vague. From *Scientific American*, March 16, 1889, page 162.

A much more practical vented barrel could be made using traditional cooperage techniques as shown in figure 6-16. In this case, the edges of the staves are hollowed out on both ends.

Figure 6-16. Vented barrel. Some products such as fruits, potatoes and onions shipped better in a barrel that allowed air to circulate. George Skidmore of Chicage, Illinois, made a machine to shave both ends of a stave thereby ventilating a barrel. From Cope, page 172.

A barrel to ship wine or other liquors in bottles was the invention of S. Strauss of Charlestown, South Carolina. A stationary center shelf allowed bottles to be loaded from each end, while separating boards B and C kept the bottles safely apart. Finally, the head secured the bottles into the barrel (see figure 6-17).

Figure 6-17. Shipping barrel. Glass bottles of high-valued liquids were safely shipped inside the strudy barrel. From *Scientific American,* February 15, 1879, page 103.

HISTORY OF THE BARREL IN AMERICA

Hoops for barrels and other wooden containers were initially made from wood. Elm was a favorite because of its strength, but as the supply of elm became exhausted, iron bands were used. Later, steel wire twisted on the ends to form a circle became the preferred hoop for small slack containers such as nail kegs. As the wood shrunk when dry, the hoops could be driven to a wider section of the container, keeping the staves close together.

Adolph Eiselein of Waconia, Minnesota, patented what he claimed was a better solution. Hoops of wire bent into a serpentine configuration functioned much like a spring, always keeping the container pulled together despite swelling or shrinking of the stave width. The design is shown in figure 6-18.

Figure 6-18. Novel barrel hoop. Using a wire bent into a serpentine form functions like a spring and adjust for small changes in the container's circumference. From *Scientific American,* November 8, 1879, page 291.

Most barrels were one-way containers since it was cheaper to dispose of the barrel at its destination rather than ship it back and have it refilled. Robert F. Adams of Chariton, Iowa, hoped to change

THOSE INVENTIVE AMERICANS

that practice by constructing a "knockdown barrel." It had always been possible to knock down a barrel into its staves, hoops, and heads, but the reassembly required a skilled cooper. Adams invented a simpler approach in which the staves were held in place with nails attached to the quarter hoops, and the hoops were cut to produce a pair of barrel sections. Installing chime hoops on either end and one on the bilge would reassemble the barrel. Adams' design is shown in figure 6-19.

Figure 6-19. Knockdown barrel. By using permanently nailed hoops segments, Fig. 1, the staves could be held together, and the barrel sections could be reassembled into a complete unit, Fig 2. From *Scientific American*, March 11, 1882, page 147.

These are but a few of the inventions for barrels produced by creative Americans. With the prevalence of containers, and preoccupation with developing improvements, it becomes easier to understand how the barrel became an important part of our language, which will be discussed in Chapter 9.

[1] *Scientific America* began publication in 1845 and covered significant or noteworthy inventions.
[2] The pail always had a bail (handle) and was generally larger at the top than at the bottom.
[3] *Scientific American,* Nov. 10, 1883, p. 290.

Chapter 7
Shelburne Barrel Factory

Raymond G. Rhuland had just finished unloading a truck full of green spruce logs outside the door of his cooperage on Dock Street in Shelburne, Nova Scotia, when he was approached for an interview. Although no previous arrangements had been made with him or his wife, Donna, who both own and operate the business, the smiling proprietor graciously agreed to talk about the operation. As the interview began, he jokingly quipped to a friend who happened to pass by, "I'm going to be famous."[1]

Products Produced

The Shelburne cooperage produces two principal types of wooden containers: trawl tubs and fish-bait barrels used by local fishing fleets. The tubs, as measured on the outsides, are twenty-three inches wide at the top, eighteen inches wide on the bottom, and twenty-four inches high. Fishing boat crews use them to hold line. It is the barrel, however, that comprises most of the two to three thousand containers[2] produced by the firm each year. They are used for packing two hundred pounds of baitfish, which corresponds to a liquid capacity of thirty gallons. Each has an eighteen-inch wide (diameter) head on the top and bottom, measures twenty and one-half inches at the center bilge, and is about twenty-eight inches high.

Both containers are made liquid tight, but holes are drilled in the bottom of the tapered trawl tub to allow seawater from the lines to drain through. The barrel, though, is considerably more complex than a tub; hence, the various steps involved in its construction are the principal focus of the following description (see figure 7-1).

A barrel begins with the spruce logs Rhuland off-loaded from his truck a few minutes ago. The logs range in diameter from four to sixteen inches, but typically are about one foot wide and ten to twelve feet long. The first step is to power up a chain saw and cut the log into short, easily-handled sections, called *bolts*, which are slightly longer than the length of a finished barrel stave.

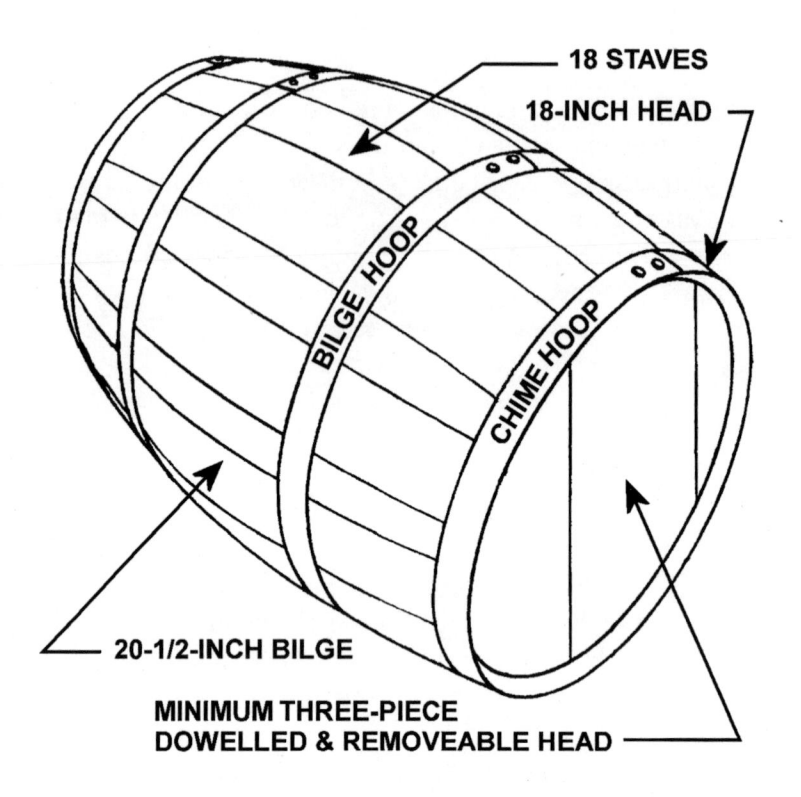

Figure 7-1. The 30-gallon or 200-pound Shelburne fish-bait barrel as produced by Raymond G. and Donna M. Rhuland in their Nova Scotia cooperage. Illustration by the author, 2004.

    The bolt is then run through a 20-inch wide (diameter) cylinder saw, which produces stave "blanks" 5/8-inches thick with the desired curvature on both the inside and outside (see figure 7-2). Staves so produced, however, are not quarter-sawn as required by coopers making barrels for oak wine casks, but this production process is completely satisfactory for what Rhuland's barrels will be used for.

SHELBURNE BARREL FACTORY

Figure 7-2. A 24-inch cylinder saw from an old tool catalog that performed the same function as a more modern 20-inch device currently used by the Shelburne Barrel Factory. From an 1887 catalog of Peter Gerlach Co. found in Kenneth Cope, *American Cooperage Machinery and Tools*, page 26. As the bolt slides by the outside of the cylinder, a stave is cut off inside and held by a "drag" that removes it when the bolt is returned to the starting position.

Next, the blank goes to the adjacent joiner where the guide has been adjusted to an angle of ten degrees to correspond to the use of eighteen staves in a barrel.[3] The blank is positioned on the guide, which slides on a slightly curving rail by the 8-inch carbide-tipped saw blade. The first pass removes the material on one edge, and a second pass on the other edge, producing a properly listed[4] and beveled stave (see figures 7-3 and 7-4).

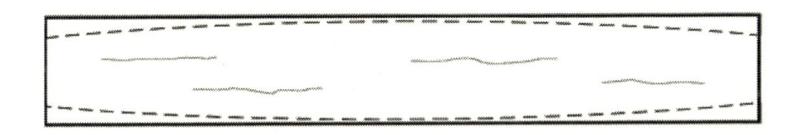

Figure 7-3. After two passes through the joiner the blank is cut into a stave with both the required correct angle and end taper for the barrel shape. Illustration by the author.

137

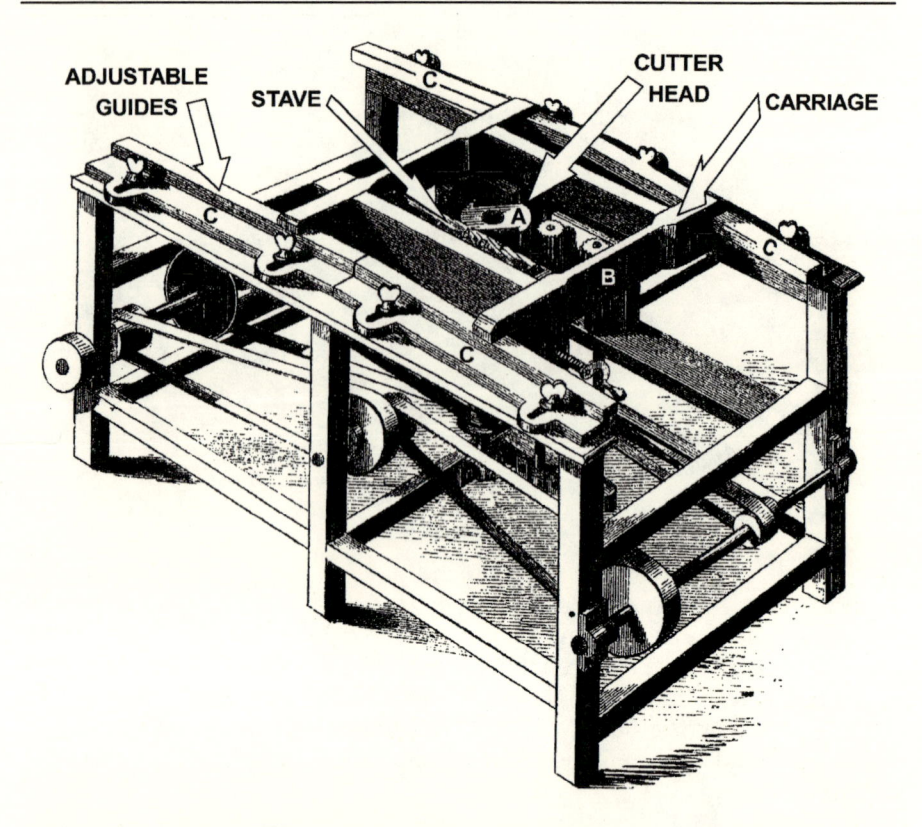

Figure 7-4. This 1859-stave joiner employs the same stave jointing and dressing principles used in Rhuland's more up-to-date saw joiner. Carriage B slides on adjustable guides C and holds a stave as it moves by the rotating cutter head A where the stave is both joined with the proper angle and dressed to the desired taper. Adapted by the author from a Benter, Burkle & Co. catalog found in Kenneth Cope, *American Cooperage Machinery Tools,* page 16.

Having been cut from wood described as "the greener the better," the staves are stacked on pallets about three per layer, with each successive layer crisscrossed with the previous to allow air to easily pass through. The pallets, generally 48 inches wide, are stored outside for about thirty days to allow the staves to dry. Rhuland noted, "The length of time depends on the weather," then added, "a moisture content of about fifteen percent is desired."[5] The "headings" (short boards for the barrel heads) are also cut to length and similarly stacked and stored outside for open-air drying.

SHELBURNE BARREL FACTORY

Raising the Barrel

The center width of the staves varies slightly, but averages about 3-9/16 (specifically 3.578) inches, requiring the previously noted quantity of eighteen to produce a barrel 20-1/2 inches wide at the bilge. To ensure the correct diameter barrel is produced, the staves can be horizontally laid side-by-side in groups of nine on a tabletop jig. Where necessary, staves of varying center dimensions can be substituted to produce the proper width for one half of a barrel.

Rhuland, however, skips this pre-sorting step, preferring to randomly select air-dried staves as they are inserted into the barrel-raising device he calls a "cradle." The device is on the opposite end of the cooperage from the cylinder saw and joiner. The staves are placed vertically side-by-side and held on the lower part by a setting up ring with an inside diameter of 18-1/4-inches made of 5/8-inch steel rod. This creates an un-trussed barrel, as shown in figure 7-5.

Figure 7-5. Cradle or barrel-raising device that holds the staves on the bottom between two bands of metal, but allows them to lean outwards against a steel setting up ring or hoop that is resting on side supports. Additional rings are shown on both sides. This is similar to the cradle used by the Shelburne Barrel Factory today. From E. & B. Holmes, Catalog Q, issued about 1915 and found in Kenneth Cope, *American Cooperage Machinery and Tools*, page 40.

Next, a steel-cable windlass, see figure 7-6, is placed around the staves and they are drawn together at the top, where a second and slightly larger setting-up ring is placed. At this point the staves are together at the bottom and partially together at the top. A cooper's adz is use to hammer any errant stave into place before the assembly is heated.

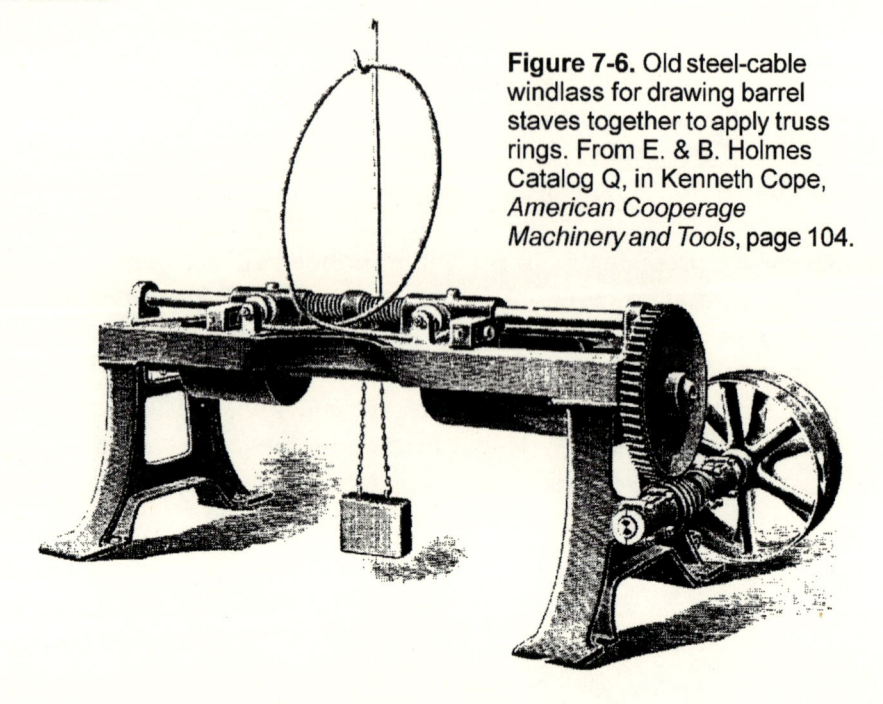

Figure 7-6. Old steel-cable windlass for drawing barrel staves together to apply truss rings. From E. & B. Holmes Catalog Q, in Kenneth Cope, *American Cooperage Machinery and Tools*, page 104.

Rhuland built his own windlass by examining similar devices found in old coopers' machinery catalogs. The one depicted in figure 7-6 is powered from a flat belt (not shown), but Rhuland constructed his windlass using hydraulic power, which provided a smoother and more reliable operation.

The next step is to heat the assembly to make the staves pliable enough to bend into the final shape. The barrel is positioned over a vertical heater about a foot wide and two feet high, and fueled by woodchips, which are the ubiquitous byproduct of cooperage (see figure 7-7). The barrel remains in place for about seven to eight minutes, becoming hot enough to char the insides of the staves in some places.

Afterward, it is removed and returned to the trussing windlass, which draws the open staves together and a second 18-1/4-inch wide setting-up ring is hammered into place. At this point, the staves are drawn together tightly and the assembly begins to look like a barrel, although both ends are still open. The staves, however, are not

SHELBURNE BARREL FACTORY

precisely even on each end and the next operation will address this imperfection.

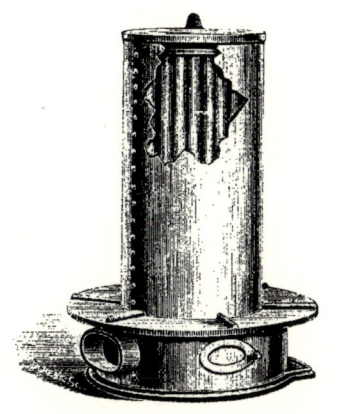

Figure 7-7. Barrel heater, which is roughly similar to the one used by the Shelburne Barrel Factory. From E. & B. Holmes Cataloge Q, found in Kenneth Cope, *American Cooperage Machinery and Tools,* page 40.

While the barrel is still hot, or at least very warm, it is moved to a nearby machine called a "forge." Through a base-mounted, multiple-head cutter, several operations are performed in one rotation of the barrel including: topping – the ends of the staves are trimmed to the same length; chiming – the top inside surface of the staves is chamfered, producing the barrel's chime; howeling – the inside of the staves below the chime is howeled to create a concave even surface for the croze; and crozing – a V-shaped groove is cut into the staves producing the croze where the head will set (see figure 7-8).

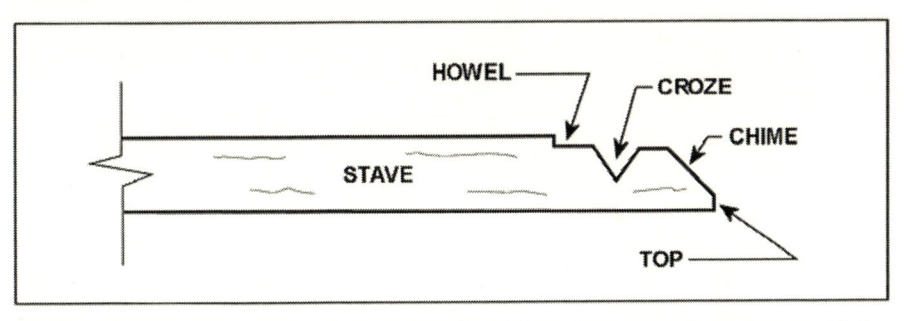

Figure 7-8. Cross-section of a stave after it has been run though a multiple-head machine Rhuland calls a forge, which produces a smooth top, the chime, the concave howel, and the V-shaped croze. Illustration by the author, 2004.

After this has been done on both ends, the inside of any exposed knot is painted with a heated mixture of one-third paraffin

HISTORY OF THE BARREL IN AMERICA

wax and two-thirds gum rosin. Over time, the knots have a tendency to develop a diagonal crack and this compound prevents leaks from occurring.

Bilge hoops made of 1-1/4-inch-wide, 16-gauge galvanized iron strap, riveted in two places and flared to the proper angle, are dropped over the setting-up rings and snugly pushed into position (see figure 7-1). The barrel is placed into Rhuland's hydraulically powered press, which forces the hoops tightly onto the staves (see figure 7-9). The process is repeated on the opposite end and the setting-up rings are then removed. As a result of a "set" that was produced by the heating, the barrel staves remain bent in place.

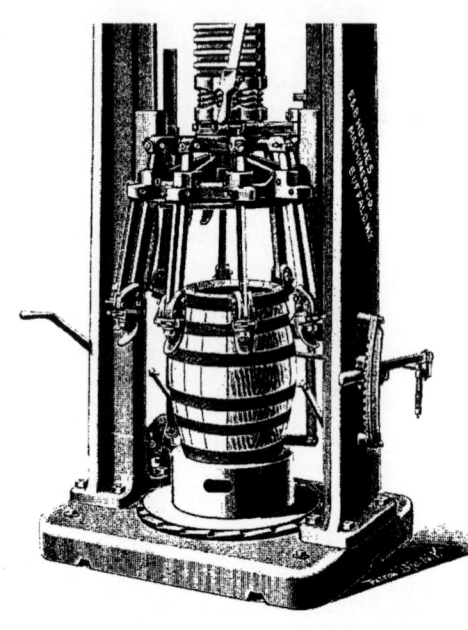

Figure 7-9. Power driver, circa 1915, for pressing hoops onto a barrel. Rhuland designed and built a hydraulic version of a similar machine, which he uses today. Portion of an illustration from E. & B. Holmes Catalog Q, taken from Kenneth Cope, *American Cooperage Machinery and Tools*, page 98.

Installation of the barrelheads and bottoms occurs at this point, but first a digression to explain how they are made.

Making Barrelheads and Bottoms

Barrelheads and bottoms consists of three or more pieces of "headings" aligned side by side and held together by two 5/16-inch birch dowels, each 2-inches long. "We never use only two headings for the top or bottom," notes Rhuland, because at least one head has

SHELBURNE BARREL FACTORY

to be removed and subsequently replaced to fill the barrel. Rhuland says the dowels keep the pieces aligned, but allow for some bowing of the head, making it easier to get it out and, afterward, to put it back. Occasionally, he produces a head with only two pieces of wood, but in these cases they find their way into the bottom of a trawl tub.

The headings are usually rectangular, but Rhuland will sometimes also use a trapezoidal piece of wood that has been sawed from a board in a way to avoid a knot or other defect. Initially, the head is assembled with three or more pieces, producing a blank that is approximately square. The assembly is then mounted on a head-cutting machine consisting of a turntable, and a dish-shaped, 11-inch saw blade with a datto head mounted on the inside. As the turntable is rotated, this combination cuts the 13/16-inch thick blank into a circle with an irregular V-shaped edge. An early version of a flat-belt driven head-cutting machine is shown in figure 7-10.

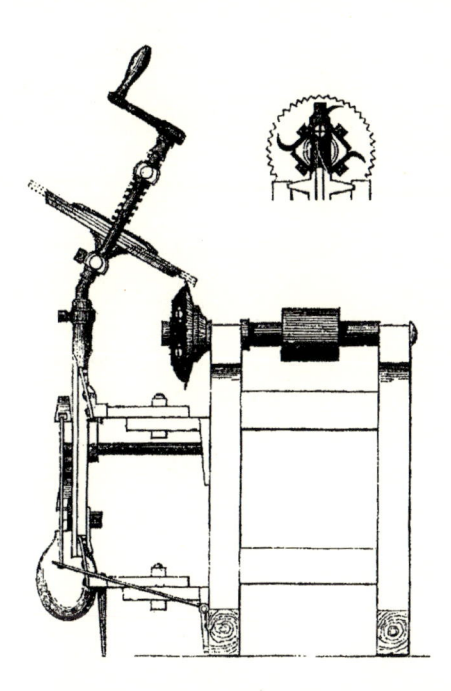

Figure 7-10. Head-making machine. The head is mounted on a turntable, which can be rotated by the handle. The combination dish-saw and datto head are driven by a flat belt to the pulley. Shown in the circle (above right) is the view of the cutting heads as seen from the left side. Adapted by the author from E. G. Brown 1851 catalog as found in Kenneth Cope, *American Cooperage Machinery and Tools*, page 19.

The V-edge has one third on the top or outside of the barrel, and two thirds on the inside (see figure 7-11). The strength of the configuration derives from the acute angle against the outside of the

HISTORY OF THE BARREL IN AMERICA

croze, as well as the increased amount of material behind the acute angle when compared with a symmetrical cut.[6]

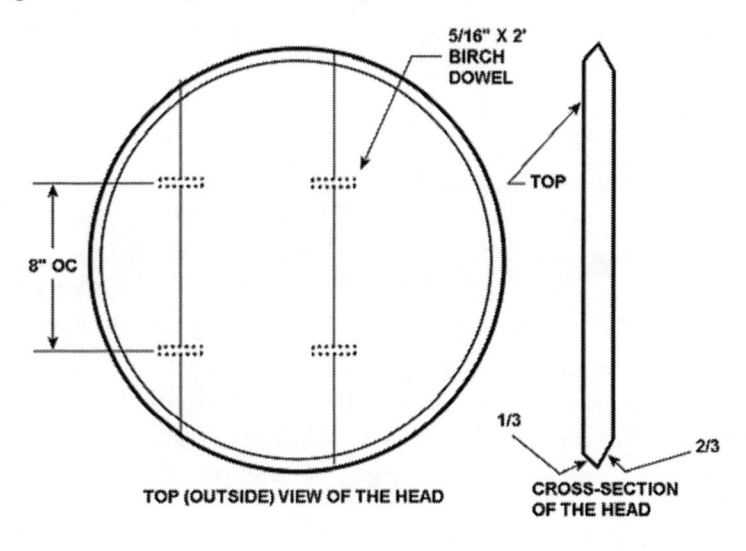

Figure 7-11. A typical three-piece Shelburne barrelhead is shown with dowel pins aligning the headings. The top (outside) of the head has a more acute angle on the bevel being shorter by a ratio of 1/3 compared the with the bottom bevel of 2/3. Illustration by the author, 2004.

Today, Rhuland buys his dowels from a supplier, but many years ago produced his own for joining the heading pieces. Using a birch log, he cut a two-inch long piece of wood and sawed it into narrow, 5/16-inch strips. The strips were then stacked seven to eight pieces high, positioned in a jig and sawed into square dowels. Rhuland likes to point out to visitors who inquire that at one time he was an expert at putting "square pegs into round holes."[7] The hard birch can be tapped into the soft spruce without too much difficulty.

Installing the Heads and Bottoms

At this stage of construction, the barrel has only the two bilge hoops in place. The setting-up rings were previously removed. It is still very warm from being heated and the staves remain close together. A bottom, however, can be slightly bowed and slipped into place. Thereafter, a hoop made of 16-gauge galvanized iron, but in this case wider at 1-5/8-inches, is pressed on.

The barrel is turned over and the head, also made of at least three heading pieces, can be also be bowed and slipped past the beveled chime and into the croze. Subsequently, the chime hoop is installed on the top of the barrel.

Sometimes there may be a slight chip in a head or bottom, which will not properly seal against the croze to produce a watertight container. In these cases, a natural gasket material called "flag" is folded and placed adjacent to the chip as the head or bottom is inserted. Any excess protruding over the chime is trimmed away with an adz.

In the fall, Rhuland gathers a supply of cat-o-nine-tail reeds that grow in marshy areas around the town. The concentric growth rings are separated, flattened, and dried. As the flag becomes wet, it swells to a greater thickness, producing an organic seal.

Testing for Leaks

Just before inserting the top head, Rhuland pours a cup of water inside the barrel. Once the head is in place, he sloshes the water around causing it to be evaporated by the latent heat present in the staves. He carefully looks for spewing steam as well as he listens for any hissing sound. Occasionally, a leak will be found, then repaired by tightening the hoops or inserting a piece of flag.

In the past, another test was used that entailed more work and was less effective. A half-inch hole was bored in the head and a mating plug was used to score an indentation in the wood, about two to three inches from the edge of the hole along the grain. This produced a slight depression in the wood that acted as a guide for the plug. The tester would then place his lips to the hole and blow into the barrel while simultaneously positioning the plug in the end of the guide. He would quickly withdraw his mouth and immediately slide the plug along the guide toward the hole, trapping a positive pressure inside the barrel. In this case, he would listen for a hissing sound to indicate a leak.

HISTORY OF THE BARREL IN AMERICA

Marking

In the eighteenth century, coopers in England were required to mark casks to certify they would hold the amount prescribed by law. Elsewhere, the proud cooper signed the cask, simply indicating he was the individual who produced it. Some of these marks were quite elaborate and took a few minutes to make.

Over the years, Rhuland developed his own distinctive style for marking the top of the barrel that was both fast and inexpensive. Using an upright adz with the handle positioned against the chime, he rotates the blade a small amount producing a segment of an arc scoured by the blade into the top of the barrel. Then, moving the adz handle to a position against the chime about thirty degrees along the circumference, he would repeat the procedure producing an X with curved sides. Today, however, he and his wife simply mark the top of the barrel with a piece of chalk. As the only coopers supplying tubs and barrels to the nearby fishing fleets, everyone knows who made the containers, and his reputation for quality keeps their company in business.

Reproduction Barrels

The cooperage occasionally makes barrels for museums. One such request came in 1988 after a Basque whaling ship that sank in 1564 was discovered. The whale oil barrels recovered were about fifty gallons, made of oak, and bound with split-sapling wooden hoops. Rhuland was able to recreate the barrel, which he bound with one-inch wide alder saplings split with an ax and smoothed on the split side with a drawknife. About twelve loops held the staves at the top and bottom of the barrel. Another order involved a group of barrels for old Ft. Niagara. But these request only come along occasionally. The mainstay of the business since they began in 1975 continues to be tubs for the long-line fishing fleet and fish-bait barrels for the lobster fleet. Asked if there were any other coopers in Canada making barrels, he said a couple make them for museums and for interpretive living history programs, but quickly noted he and his wife were "the only ones making a living out of making barrels."[8] See figures 7-12 and 7-13.

SHELBURNE BARREL FACTORY (1975) LTD.
GST #R104828082
Dock Street, P.O. Box 790
SHELBURNE, NOVA SCOTIA   BOT 1W0
(902) 875-2047

Figure 7-12. Company identification found on the top of an invoice of the Shelburne Barrel Factory in Nova Scotia, Canada.

Figure 7-13. Donna M. and Raymond G. Rhuland, coopers, owners, and operators of the Shelburne Barrel Factory in Shelburne, Nova Scotia, Canada. Photo by Alan Delaney, 2004, used by permission.

HISTORY OF THE BARREL IN AMERICA

[1] Oral history interview of Raymond G. Rhuland (b. 1949), conducted by Jack L. Shagena on August 9, 2004 at the Shelburne Barrel Factory (1975) LTD, in Shelburne, Nova Scotia, Canada.

[2] Ibid. In the "good old days" Rhuland said they produced 7- to 10-thousand containers each year. In a telephone interview with Rhuland on August 30, 2004 he explained, that before about 1979-80 the barrels were also used for food fish sent to the West Indies, Russia, and eastern Canada. At that time there was a cooperage in New Brunswick and another one in Nova Scotia each producing about 50-thousand barrels annually. A change in government food regulations caused a transition to plastic barrels and Rhuland's competition went out of business. He continued to operate by making wooden lobster traps for a while, a business that disappeared in 1990 with the introduction of plastic-covered wire. Today he survives by producing fish-bait barrels for the lobster fleet and trawl tubs for the long-line fishing fleet.

[3] Refer to the formula in Chapter 4 to determine the relationship between the number of staves and the angle.

[4] The specific amount removed on each edge after a pass through the joiner will vary, but there must be a fourteen percent difference in the end widths compared to the center to produce a barrel with a bulge of 20-1/2 inches at the bilge and 18-inches at the top, a ratio of 1:14.

[5] Oral history interview.

[6] Rhuland points out that the angle around the edge of the head must be slightly more obtuse (wider) than the angle formed by the croze V-groove otherwise the apex of the head angle will bottom out and a good seal will not be obtained on the sides. Telephone interview conducted with Raymond Rhuland on August 30, 2004.

[7] Telephone interview.

[8] Oral history interview.

Chapter 8
Brooks Barrel Company

World War II had ended, and after spending four years in the Army, Paul Brooks in 1945 headed home to Cambridge, Maryland. He and his family had deepwater roots in the Eastern Shore. As shipbuilders, his grandfather and great-grandfather from Dorchester County had more vessels on the Chesapeake Bay than any other shipbuilder until the late 1800s, and his mother's family from Hooper Island had been in the seafood packing business for many years. His father had also worked in the marine business operating shipyard repair facilities.

Following the war, however, his dad decided to open a lumberyard to supply local shipbuilders materials to replenish the fishing and oyster workboats that had been repaired and patched during the last half decade. Paul took a job with his father, but notes, "I did not particularly care for the sawmill business."[1] So using a portion of his father's mill property, and going against the advice of friends and family, he decided to start a barrel business.

Establishing the Barrel Company

"Barrels were coming into use for seafood so I took a little survey,"[2] reported Brooks, who found out where to buy barrelheads, staves, and hoops. Then he found "some boys from Virginia" who had experience in making potatoes barrels and in January 1950 the new enterprise was opened. His initial customer was the nearby seafood industry that in the winter packed oysters, and in the summer, crabs.

The business soon needed to expand to keep pace with the demand. When the brand-new Ivy and Jennings Tomato Cannery outside of Cambridge on Bucktown Road burned down about 1953, he acquired three parcels of land amounting to just under five acres. The site had formerly been the location of Thompson Station, served by a spur of the Maryland and Delaware Railroad that went from

HISTORY OF THE BARREL IN AMERICA

Cape Charles to Wilmington. Brooks built a structure and with the help of Frank Knox, a cooper and "old bachelor" from Melfa (Accomack County), Virginia, Ed Bailey of Milton, Delaware, and Elzy Burton of Cambridge, his business grew. He noted, "They [Knox, Bailey and Burton] liked to make barrels."

Adjusting to Supplier Problems

It was not too long, however, when his barrelhead supplier in Virginia went out of business. Brooks set up a sawmill plant in east Cambridge to turn out his own barrelheads, which consisted of three individual pieces of wood. Later, he would acquire a machine specifically designed to make the heads and install it in the factory on Bucktown Road.

His next problem arose when his stave supplier went barrel-belly up. One piece of equipment, a stave mill, was obtained from a chicken processing plant in Berlin, Maryland, that no longer made its own barrels. He subsequently acquired machinery "from all over" the country and produced his own staves as well as staves for other cooperages assembling barrels. Some of these were potato farmers who, in the winter would make barrels and store the empty containers in their barns. At harvest time, they would fill them with potatoes and ship the barrels to market on the railroad.

Brooks' third and last major problems with suppliers occurred when American Wire and Steel Company, which made wire hoops, and Acme Steel Company in Chicago, which made flat steel hoops, went out of business. Acme offered to give Brooks its equipment if he would remove it. So he took a trip to the windy city and visited the plant, recalling, "I looked at that mess and said 'holy cow'!"[3] Initially he had considered renting a U-haul truck and driving the equipment back to Cambridge, but it was too much. So he hired truckers who delivered two trailer loads to his plant on Bucktown Road. A machine for riveting the end of a flat steel barrel hoop is shown in figure 8-1.

To make his own wire hoops, he bought machines from an out-of-business cooperage in Arkansas. At the same time he acquired 15- and 20-inch cylinder saws for producing staves for both barrels and kegs. One barrel he made in the 1950s, and that is still produced today, is the U.S. standard size of 7,056 cubic inches, 17-1/8-inches wide at the head with staves 28-1/2-inches long.[4] The smaller keg was used as a shipping container for nuts, bolts, railroad spikes, and nails. "At one time in the late 1960s we were really jumping"[5] he recalled, as both the barrel business and selling staves to a cooperage in Crisfield, Maryland, was very good.

Figure 8-1. Paul Brooks is shown riveting together the ends of a barrel hoop made of steel. Photograph taken by Jean Firth Tyng about 1955 and used with permission of Franklin Tyne.

In 1962, a newspaper article reported the Brooks cooperage was turning out 50,000 barrels per year of eight different sizes ranging from 18 to 36 inches high and from 14 to 24 inches wide. Seafood and meatpackers were buying barrels for $1.65 each and they were delivered by truck with special rack bodies that could carry 180 barrels.

HISTORY OF THE BARREL IN AMERICA

The work force consisted of six men in addition to Brooks and chief cooper Frank Knox, who writer Walter E. Huelle describes:

> "[He] is in perpetual motion as he works, using his knees to help keep the staves in line as he drops them into a forming ring, he reaches now to the left and now to the right to pick up more. By hand he loops the wire over the flared-out ends and then winds a turnbuckle to pull them together. An adze that resembles a tomahawk serves him to tap the hoops in place, and a hand crozer to cut the grooves in the barrel end. Yet so skillful is he that he can make 60 barrels in a day, and had been turning out about 10,000 a year, barrels so tight that although they are not actually designed to hold liquids, once they have swollen they will do so.[6]

Frank Knox had previously earned a living making potato barrels on the eastern shore of Virginia, but was working for a sawmill prior to coming to work for Paul Brooks in the early part of the 1950s. Brooks recalled, "He was tickled to death to get back in the barrel business" [7] (see figure 8-2).

Changing Business Patterns

Brooks observes that once it was learned to "steam crabs and eat them like lobster in the early 1960s" they became more popular. Gradually the crab-shipping container transitioned from the barrel to the cheaper wooden bushel basket. In the Eastern Shore poultry industry as well, the barrel was replaced by the more sanitary hot-wax-dipped, wire-bound crates, and later by the plastic-lined cardboard boxes. As these changes evolved in the marketplace, Brooks had to find new business opportunities.

During the 1970s, he sold many barrels to the meat-packing industry in Philadelphia. The local barrel manufacturers who had produced "flour and sugar barrels went by the wayside," so he started taking his containers north and returning with old slack barrels called "spreaders." The top hoop and head had been removed to allow the staves to flair open and a number of spreaders were stacked one inside the other, allowing a larger number of containers to be transported at one time. These were re-coopered in Cambridge and returned to Philadelphia, where they were packed with beef products and shipped to processing plants to make hamburger, sausage, and hotdogs.

BROOKS BARREL COMPANY

Figure 8-2 Cooper, Frank Knox is shown making a barrel by hand, and is credited as "a big part of getting the company going." [8] The wheel on the right is part of a windlass that is turned to draw the staves together. Photograph taken by Jean Firth Tyng about 1955 and used with permission of Franklin Tyne.

Brooks also expanded his marketing reach by using sales representatives to sell his barrels at distant locations such as the Pottery Factory in Williamsburg, Virginia. In addition he acquired a nailing machine and made wooden boxes, specifically for field peas. As technology and business patterns changed he recalled, "I had to do a lot myself to figure it out."[9]

In a 1974 interview with the *Evening Sun* in Baltimore, Brooks stated the company was producing 60,000 barrels per year for the seafood, meatpacking, and wholesale shipping markets, using equipment described as "a collection of antiques." It was specifically noted that oysters sold on the half-shell were shipped in barrels. The company had twelve employees, and Brooks was not eager to expand the business, philosophically stating:

You like to make all the money you can, and we did try expanding once, but it got to the point where I was knocking myself out to make an extra buck.

First you've got to hire more people and it's a job finding workers anymore that don't mind getting their hands messed up. And then, if you hire more workers, you've got to hire more managers, and soon you're running a business sort of second hand or third hand.

I like to keep my fingers on things.[10]

Ken Knox Joins Brooks Barrel

As a child growing in the mid-1950s to 60s, Ken Knox exhibited a keen aptitude for mechanical devices. So much so, he acknowledged, "My mother would give me a hard time because I would take thing apart and put them back together." Asked if he ever took a vacuum cleaner apart he chuckled and responded, "No, I didn't want to get that close to something I might have to use."[11] Little did the youngster realize that his innate curiosity about how things worked would play a major role in his chosen career many years later.

After growing up in Cambridge, Knox served in the U.S. military, after which he returned home and worked as a medical laboratory technician. In April 1798, at age twenty-four, he went to work for Paul Brooks at the barrel company with the intention of learning the business and eventually acquiring the company. Starting at the bottom, Knox learned the idiosyncrasies of each piece of oily dust-covered antique piece of equipment – how to sharpen blades and knives, how to fix the machines when they broke, and how to keep them running in-between. He describes himself as a "jack of all trades, master of none," remaining in the office only when he has to, otherwise he is a hands-on person out on the floor gravitating to wherever there may be a problem.

With Brooks as his mentor, he became proficient in every aspect of making wooden barrels, tubs, and buckets, and along the way the company acquired more vintage equipment as other cooperages went out of business. In some cases, the machinery was put to work, while other pieces are still retained as a future source of spare parts. "We have enough excess machinery that we could start another company," noted Knox, who added the business "probably own more barrel [cylinder] saws than any other slack cooperage."[12]

Knox Buys the Business

In 1991, he acquired the company and continued to operate it the same way Paul Brooks had done for years. He did, however, institute one minor change with regard to the timber that goes into barrels. Heretofore the company had harvested trees in the nearby forest, cutting poplar, gum, and pine for its wooden products. Knox decided to buy logs on the open market and found pine the most available, so he switched to it almost exclusively (see figure 8-3).

Figure 8-3. Ken Knox, President of Brooks Barrel Company, stands in front of a stack of wire-hooped slack shipping barrels ready to be delivered to a customer. The company produces about thirty different types of wooden containers – primarily tubs, buckets, kegs, and barrels. He also will provide his customers bushel-type baskets, which he obtains from another supplier. Photo by Jack Shagena, 2004.

"Around 1998," Knox said, "I got away from the old barrel [cylinder] saws as it was getting hard to find people to put a new face on them; to do one saw was $5,000 and there was no guarantee." He did have one done, but the blade did not last forty hours, so he decided to install a more modern and safer planing mill. "The cylinder machinery I designed and had built," he noted, and "some of it [the mill] I bought and redesigned to do what I wanted to do."[13] It was expensive – before the project was complete he had spent upward of a quarter-million dollars – but says the capital investment was needed to stay in business.

Most of the machinery he uses is about twice as old as he is. He is proud of every piece, noting, "You have heard the old expression they don't make thing like they used to," and after receiving an approving nod continues, "we have those old things here." Even today he remains impressed with the "tremendous amount of thought" that went into the designs, explaining "the people who invented these machines had it together – really knew what they were doing."[14]

Perhaps Knox's most impressive equipment is a five-in-one machine manufactured by E. & B. Holmes of Buffalo, New York, around 1900. As the name implies, it accomplishes five operations in one piece of equipment: truing up a recently-trussed barrel so it does not lean one way or the other and pressing the hoops into place; cutting off the top of the staves so they are all of an equal height; chamfering the chime on the top inside edge of the barrel; producing a concave channel (howel) around the inside of the top just below the chime; and cutting a V-groove or croze into the howel to accept the barrelhead (see figure 8-4).

Once this has been done on both ends, the head is installed by loosening the top or chime hoop, dropping in the head, and pressing the hoop back into place. To keep the head from falling into the barrel, Knox uses a discarded automobile engine valve where the stem has been sharpened to function as a pick that is stabbed into the barrelhead.

Figure 8-4. Catalog illustration of the five-in-one machine used by the Brooks Barrel Company. From E. & B. Holmes catalog S, page 94.

The Company Today

Under Ken Knox's leadership the business has grown considerably, producing 75,000 to 100,000 wooden containers each year. Many are shipping barrels of various sizes but the company's thirty or so products include items for the lawn and garden, kegs for confectioners showcasing candy, barrels for coffee beans, and display barrels for pseudo-country stores, breweries, and wineries and occasionally a movie set.

He is constantly looking for new opportunities. Not too long ago he began discussions with an aerospace company to produce 500,000 barrels for an undisclosed requirement. After the initial euphoria wore off, he concluded the contract would significantly strain his operation, requiring three shifts per day to turn them out on schedule. He was much relieved the company found another way to satisfy its requirement.

The future for slack cooperages throughout the country has not been bright. A hundred years ago, there was a barrel-maker in nearly every small town where the local population produced a product that was shipped in bulk. Knox remembers when he came to work at Brooks in 1978, there were only six slack cooperages in the country. In 2004, the number had dropped to three. The others are in Maine, but Brooks is the only one who continues to produce the "authentic nail keg."

Despite the company's prosperity, there are those occasional very difficult days at the antiquated sprawling non-descript barrel factory on Bucktown Road. He says, "Sometimes I look up at the heavens and say 'you are testing me aren't you'?"[15]

Much of the company's success derives from his work ethic of doing any task, including sweeping the floor, to promote the efficiency of the operation. From his military experience, he says with conviction, "I believe in looking out for my people; they are my assets and without them everything else is irrelevant."[16]

---

[1] Telephone interview with Paul Brooks (b. July 31, 1922) on Oct. 31, 2004 by Jack L. Shagena.
[2] Ibid.
[3] Ibid.
[4] This produces a barrel with 26 inches between the heads and outside circumference of about 64 inches (see table 5-2).
[5] Interview with Brooks.
[6] Walter E. Huelle, "Barrels for the Crabs of Maryland, a Shore Plant Makes 50,000 a Year for Seafood and Meat Packers," *Baltimore Sun*, May 20, 1962
[7] Interview with Brooks
[8] Interview with Ken Knox (b. 1954) on Oct. 28, 2005 at the Brooks Barrel Company in Cambridge, MD.
[9] Ibid.
[10] Frank Megaree, "Logs Go in One End Of Cooperage On The Shore, Finished Barrel Come Rolling Out The Other," *Baltimore Evening Sun* Feb. 15, 1974.
[11] Interview with Knox.
[12] Ibid.
[13] Ibid. Both quotes in the paragraph.
[14] Ibid. Both quotes in the paragraph.
[15] Earlier telephone conservation with Ken Knox on Oct. 13, 2004.
[16] Interview with Knox.

Chapter 9
Barrels: Integrated into Our Culture

The American language is rich with barrel expressions and this came about from the millions of barrels that were commonplace on the landscape for more than three hundred years. As early as 1791, Alexander Hamilton, Secretary of the Treasury, reported to the Congress on manufactures, noting a "vast scene of household manufacturing" and specifically pointing out, "Ships, cabinet wares, and turpentine; . . [and] cooper' wares of every kind . . ." are contributing "more largely to the community than could be imagined without having made it an object of particular inquiry."[1]

As America expanded and the population grew, barrels kept pace as bulk containers for flour, beer, pork, and grain of every kind. To understand the omnipresence of barrels during the early part of the 1900s, table 9-1 is presented.

Table 9-1. The U.S. cumulative population increase from 1906 to 1910 along with the slack barrels and kegs produced. Population from U.S. census, and the barrel information from Coyne, page 39.

Year	U.S. Pop. (Million)	Cum. U.S. Pop. Growth (Million)	Yearly Barrels (Million)	Cum. Barrels (Million)
1905	83.8	-	-	-
1906	85.5	1.7	68	68
1907	87.0	3.2	74	142
1908	88.7	4.9	97	239
1909	90.5	6.7	127	366
1910	92.4	8.6	91	457

From 1906 through 1910, the United States produced 457 million slack barrels and kegs while the population grew 8.6 million.

HISTORY OF THE BARREL IN AMERICA

This represented an increase in barrels of more than fifty times the population growth. Ignoring the number of barrels in existence in 1905, and assuming the barrels afterward survived the five-year period, this would have meant there were almost five barrels per person in the United States in 1910. Actually many of the barrels were used to export American goods, but as products were also imported in barrels, most likely this produced a reasonably close offset.

Advertising

One of the reasons Americans remembered barrels was through advertising. America's first product was tobacco and an ad run by a New York City store is shown in figure 9-1.

Figure 9-1. Advertisement promoting chewing tobacco is shown along with barrels or hogsheads. From Robert K. Heimann, *Tobacco and Americans* (New York: McGraw-Hill, 1960), page 190.

Barrel images were used for wholesalers, since many of the products sold were packed in the containers (see figure 9-2).

BARRELS: INTEGRATED INTO OUR CULTURE

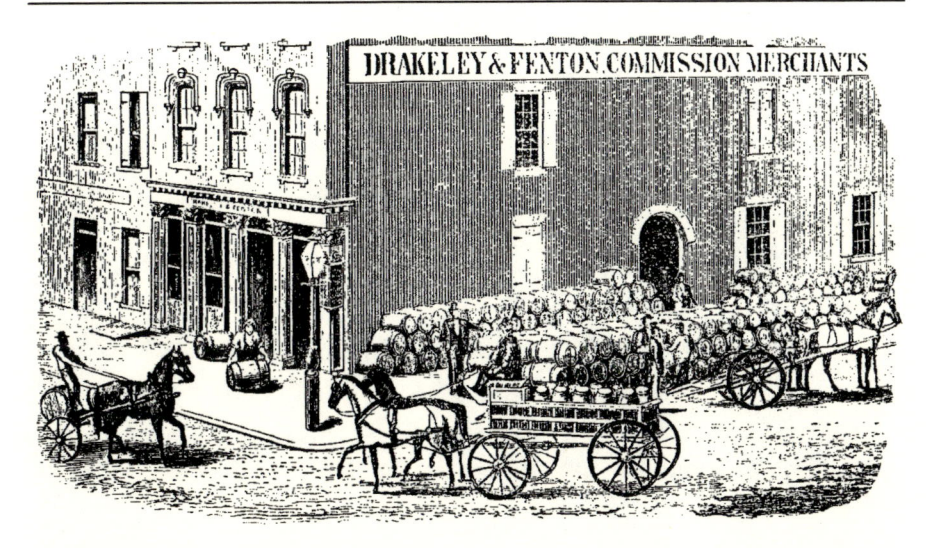

Figure 9-2. A commission merchant of provisions and produce in Baltimore, Drakeley & Fenton, is shown with barrels on the side of their building. A portion of an image from George W. Howard, *The Monumental City* (Baltimore: J. D. Ehlers, 1873), page 108.

Another wooden barrel example, which advertised swine medicine, can be seen in figure 9-3.

Figure 9-3. Mess Pork hog medicine of 1884 features a barrel wraped around, and no doubt protecting, the porker. From Hal Morgan, *Symbols of America*, (Rutherford, NJ: Penguin, 1987), page 75.

Promulgation of the barrel image also occurred on currency issued by the Commonwealth of Virginia. It had the same effect of keeping the container ever-present in the public's eye (see figure 9-4).

HISTORY OF THE BARREL IN AMERICA

Figure 9-4. State of Virginia, the Bank of the Commonwealth five-dollar note shows two men in hats inspecting tobacco above a barrel. From Heimann, page 79.

As late as 1901 the barrel was included on a bond certificate as a symbol of progress (see figure 9-5).

Figure 9-5. Image from a $10,000 bond of the Reading Company.

Port Scenes

A woodcut featuring barrels, bails, and boxes used on letterheads of commercial shippers is shown in figures 9-6 and 9-7. In a variety of atlases and textbooks, shipping scenes of various ports

162

BARRELS: INTEGRATED INTO OUR CULTURE

depicted barrels in the foreground with the sailing vessels in the distance (see figure 9-8).

Figure 9-6. Woodcut image used by merchants on invoices. From Stephen O. Saxe, ed., *Old-Time Advertising Cuts and Typography*, (New York: Dover, 1989), page 93.

Figure 9-7. Woodcut image that also found use on invoices. From Saxe, ed., page 93.

HISTORY OF THE BARREL IN AMERICA

Figure 9-8. Shipping port on the on the lower part of Quebec City. From S. G. Goodrich, *Pictorial History of the United Sates* (Philadelphia: E. H. Butler, 1864), page 452.

The BIBLE, the Bard, and the Barrel

Barrels and images of barrels were found everywhere, so it is understandable how expressions about the omnipresent container found their way into the American language. Probably the first book most seventeenth, eighteenth, and nineteenth century Americans saw and learned to read was the 1611 King James Version of the BIBLE. In I Kings, XVII, is written "I have not a cake, but an handful of meal in a barrel, and a little oil in cruse." Also in the same chapter we find, "And the barrel of meal wasted not, neither did the cruse of oil." [2]

It may have been comforting for the readers to be able to relate their everyday lives to these passages, however, in the 1952 Revised Standard Version, the translations were different. "I have nothing baked, only a handful of meal in a jar, and a little oil in a cruse;" and "The jar of meal was not spent, and the cruse of oil not fail."

This may raise questions about the antiquity of the word "barrel," but not about its relevance to Americans for the first three

164

BARRELS: INTEGRATED INTO OUR CULTURE

hundred years. Certainly in the time of William Shakespeare, the word was definitely known. In *Henry VI*, ca. 1591, this passage occurs in part 1, Act V, scene iv., line 57:

> Place barrels of pitch upon the fatal stake,
> That so her torture may be shortened.[3]

Also about the same time, Robert Fabyan, who died in 1513, is credited with, "The Duke of Clarence . . . then being a prisoner in the Tower, was secretly put to death and drowned in a barrel of Malmesey wine within the said Tower."[4]

Barrel Idioms

These idioms or sayings found in the American language are arranged alphabetically beginning with the most common first word.[5]

Barreling down the road. Going fast and implying somewhat out of control (see figure 9-9).

Figure 9-9. A rather bemused little girl stands by as a youngster rolls a barrel of flour, supposedly being pulled by a fellow playmate and a dog. From a Washburn Crosby trade card about 1900.

Barrel Fever. An affliction usually resulting in death from drinking too much. *He died of barrel fever.*

Barrel lot. Today, the auctioneer would likely refer to a number of small items jumbled together as a "box lot," but years ago the miscellaneous collection would have likely been placed in a wooden container and called a barrel lot.

Bottom of the barrel. The dregs or least desirable part of the barrel's contents. If my father purchased an item that failed to achieve expectations, such as paint that did not cover well, he would remark it was made from ingredient from the bottom of the barrel, meaning inferior. (Also see scrape the bottom of the barrel).

Cash on the barrelhead. No credit extended. During the days of the country general store, a barrel often would be turned upside down and used as a table for playing checkers, or perhaps at a bar for serving drinks. If the patrons could not be trusted to pay afterward, they had to first put money on the top (upright head) of the barrel.

Empty barrels make the most noise. An old English proverb suggests individuals, who have limited knowledge about a subject, are prone to expound the most. In a loosely coupled vein, the New York Yankees, during the time of Babe Ruth, were in a hitting slump. So the story goes, the manager arranged to have a wagonload of noisy empty barrels driven by the players as they departed the baseball stadium after a game. The theory being, each rattling empty barrel represented a hit, and supposedly the team was soon hitting and winning again. This particular story, however, can't be found in a number of books on baseball superstition and legend.

Fishing in a barrel. Pursuing a direction or activity deemed to be stupid or fruitless. *His perpetual motion machine was like fishing in a rain barrel* (see figure 9-10).

In the barrel. A slang expression attributed to African American use meaning without money. Also alludes to having no cloths to wear, hence donning a barrel.[6]

Like shooting fish in a barrel. Ridiculously easy, such as *coming up with ideas for writing a book is like shooting fish in a barrel.* Writing a book, however, requires the invocation of another saying, *blood, sweat, and tears.*

BARRELS: INTEGRATED INTO OUR CULTURE

Figure 9-10. A man is fishing in a rain barrel as a youngster looks on in amusement. From J. L. Nichols, *The Business Guide; or Safe Methods of Business* (Naperville, IL: J. L. Nichols, 1902), page 28.

More fun than a barrel of monkeys. Very amusing or diverting, like playing *"kick the can" is more fun than a barrel of monkeys*. The expression is a reference to the playful nature of primates. It has also been used as the name of a game in which monkeys are linked together to form chains (see figure 9-11).

Over a barrel. In a difficult, helpless or compromising position, often the result of having little or no money. W*ith the fire destroying the plant, the management is over a barrel in finding resources to rebuild.*

Rotten apple spoils the barrel. My mother used to caution me as a youngster to choose my friends carefully, since *one bad apple spoils the barrel*. The allusion is to fungi easily spreading from one piece of fruit to another when confined in close quarters.

HISTORY OF THE BARREL IN AMERICA

Figure 9-11. A barrel of monkeys having fun from an unused, undated, and un-copyrighted color post card from around the 1950s.

Scrape the bottom of the barrel. This is generally used in the sense to employ the least desirable part of the barrel's contents. My father, when purchasing an item that was at the limit of his financial resources, would remark to the salesman, "Guess I will have to go home and scrape the bottom of the barrel to get the money."

Barrel Nouns and Adjectives

In addition to idioms, barrel is used as a noun and adjective in the American language.

Barrel cactus. A barrel cactus is un-branched and has a globular-to-columnar structure.

BARRELS: INTEGRATED INTO OUR CULTURE

Barrel chair. A padded chair resembling a portion of a barrel in which the back retains the full barrel height, but about three-quarters of the front top has been removed, providing a high back. Legs have been added raising the cushioned seat to a more comfortable distance above the floor. In some cases, only half of front part was removed and a padded seat placed in the lower one-half, thus eliminating the legs (see figure 9-12).

Figure 9-12. Barrel chair. Photo by the author, 2004.

Barrel distortion. In an optical lens, barrel or pincushion distortion results in an image bulging in the middle.

Barrel drum. A barrel without heads and where the ends are covered with a thin diaphragm, often of leather, to produce a musical instrument (see figure 9-13).[7]

Barrel jumping. Usually associated with ice-skating where an individual leaps over a number of empty barrels arranged, bilge-to-bilge, in a straight line. Should the jump not be long enough, the skater would normally land on a barrel, which would most likely collapse and help break the fall.

Yvon Jolin holds the world record of 29 feet 5 inches over eighteen barrels at Terrerbonne, Quebec, Canada on January 25, 1981. Janet Hainstock holds the women's record of 20 feet 4-1/2 inches over eleven barrels set in Wyandotte, Michigan, on March 15, 1980. For skateboarding, eighteen-year-old Tony Alva jumped 17 feet over seventeen barrels at the World Professional Championship in Long Beach, California on September 25, 1977.[8]

HISTORY OF THE BARREL IN AMERICA

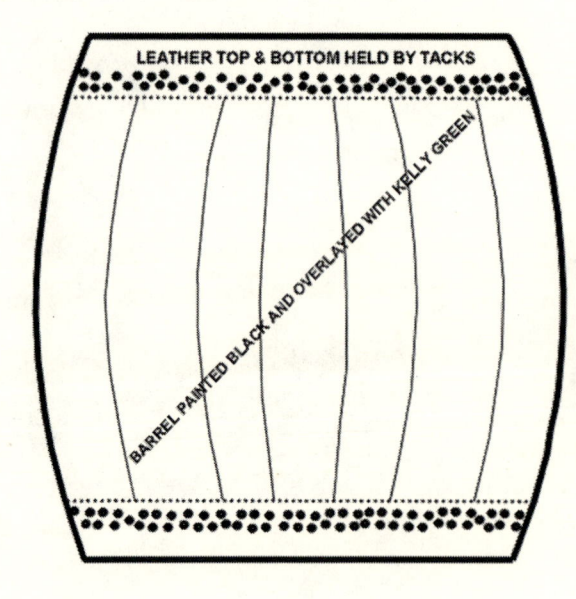

Figure 9-13. Barrel drum is 17-3/8" at the heads, 21-5/8" high, with a bilge of 22". Owned by Keith and Debbie Davidson and found at Packing House Antiques, Corp. in Cambridge, MD. Illustration by the author, 2004.

Barrel knot. A decorative knot that resembles the shape of a barrel (see figure 9-14).

Figure 9-14. Barrel knot tied using a braided nylon line. Knot tied and image scanned by the author.

Barrel of a baseball bat. The upper portion of the bat the batter wants to hit the pitched ball (see figure 9-14).

BARRELS: INTEGRATED INTO OUR CULTURE

Figure 9-15. Fan Taz, the drink of the baseball fans. The "sweet spot" on the bat, where the ball is desired to impact, is around the word "drink." From *Symbols of America*, page 67.

Barrel of a pen. The long portion of a pen gripped by the writer. (see figure 9-15).

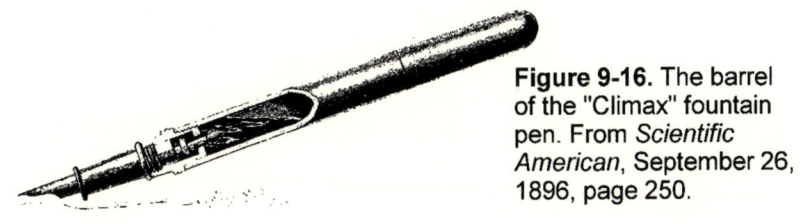

Figure 9-16. The barrel of the "Climax" fountain pen. From *Scientific American*, September 26, 1896, page 250.

Barrel organ. A type of preprogrammed musical instrument that is mechanically operated by turning a crank. The turning motion pumps a bellow and also rotates a drum or barrel that is fitted with pins. The pins momentarily open valves allowing the moving air to vibrate reeds thereby producing music.

Barrel racing. A type of timed horse racing where the rider navigates a steed around a prescribed course, originally defined by barrels. Today, empty 55-gallon drums are used.

Barrel roll. While flying an aircraft a pilot makes a complete rotation around its longitudinal axis.

HISTORY OF THE BARREL IN AMERICA

Barrel-chested. Usually an older male exhibiting a large distended abdomen and chest, hence, resembling a barrel shape. The barrel-chested man on the right is decidedly skeptical about the "deal" being offered by the slick-looking salesman. From Nichols, page 298.

Figure 9-17

Barrelhouse. Originally a barrelhouse was a low-class, or bottom of the barrel, drinking establishment where liquor was served directly from a barrel. Later, it became synonymous with cheap saloons and second-rate brothels and boarding houses.[9]

Barrelhouse music. A type of music played in drinking establishments and brothels. Storyville (the legal red-light district in New Orleans) opened in 1897 and provided musicians such as pianist "Jelly Roll" Morton well-paying jobs.[10]

Pork barrel. Government funding of a project or activity that is directed at benefiting a specific political subdivision represented by an individual who takes credit for the expenditure thereby winning political favor and being re-elected. It is a reference to the fatness of pork and the ease with which public money can be used for political purposes.

Rain barrel. A barrel used to retain rainwater draining from the roof of a structure, often a dwelling. Usually there was a temporary bypass where the initial water was diverted to the ground until the roof had been washed off, thereafter the rainwater filling the container.

BARRELS: INTEGRATED INTO OUR CULTURE

Barrel Quotations

James Barron: [With] a unique blend of Beethoven and the Beer Barrel Polka, Liberace charmed millions . . .

Anna Julia Cooper: . . . women are more quiet. They don't feel called to mount a barrel and harangue by the hour every time they imagine they have produced an idea . . . (see figure 9-18).

Figure 9-18. Standing on a barrel to preach to anyone who will listen. From Alma White, Gems of Life (Zarephath, NJ: *Pillars of Fire*, 1907), page 71.

Dale Curry: Maria Babin, a native of Karlsruhe who moved to New Orleans in 1948, still recalls her mother's homemade sauerkraut: marinate in stone pots or wooden barrels for up to a year.

J.P. Donleavy: When I die I want to decompose in a barrel of porter and have it served in all the pubs in Dublin.

Figure 9-19. A barrel of porter perhaps large enough to hold J. P. Donleavy.

HISTORY OF THE BARREL IN AMERICA

Francis D. Gage: I was born a mechanic, and made a barrel before I was ten years old. The cooper told my father, "Fanny made that barrel, and had done it quicker . . ."

Kentucky Fried Chicken: Buy a bucket of chicken and have a barrel of fun.

Lane Kirkland: [Don't] get into an argument with people who buy ink by the barrel (see figure 9-20)

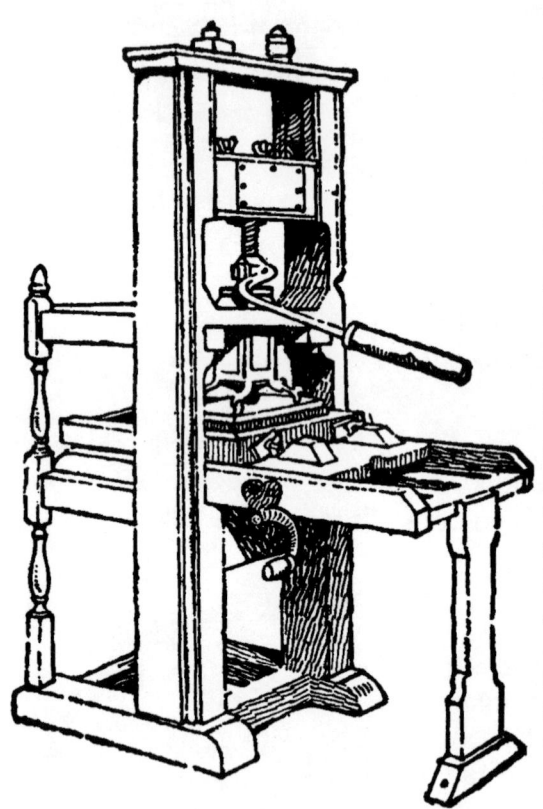

Figure 9-20. Printers for many years purchased black ink by the barrel and always have had a lot to say on the editorial page and sometimes on the front page of their papers. It is a prudent individual who recognizes this and does not try to debate an issue with a newspaper editor. From Wilber F. Gordy, *Elementary History of the United States* (New York: Charles Scribner's Sons, 1913), page 164.

Republican party: Don't change barrels going over Niagara. (Slogan satirically attributed to the Republicans during the presidential campaign of 1932.)[11]

BARRELS: INTEGRATED INTO OUR CULTURE

Gore Vidal: Television is now so desperately hungry for material they are scraping the top of the barrel.

Elinor Wylie: Peaches grow wild, and pigs live in clover; A barrel of salted herring lasts a year; The spring begins before the winter's over.

The Cracker Barrel

Perhaps the best-known expression about a barrel involves its capacity to transport crackers to an old country store where they were weighed and sold to consumers by the pound. In the store, groups of villagers, often old men, were frequently seen sitting around a pot-bellied stove surrounded by barrels containing a variety of every imaginable commodity, including the always-present cracker barrel. They would tell stories and have convincing answers to the most difficult social, financial, and political problems of the day. This common sense or conventional wisdom pontificating took on a special meaning that is still associated with the cracker barrel (see figure 9-21).[12]

In 1981, Allan Dale, a plainspoken Texan, collected his provocatively titled radio commentaries into a book that was aptly called *Cracker Barrel Comments*. One of his stories railed against the adoption of the metric system with this heading, "The Metric System . . . The Government's 373.42 G. of Flesh" and contained the following:

> Okay, so be it. But I want to ask the pundits from those great marble halls on the Potomac, what are you going to do with the following terms in our language? "Every inch a King. I love you a bushel and a peck. Penny-wise and pound foolish. God's little acre. Foot-loose and fancy free. The inch-worm. Denver, the mile high city. An ounce of prevention is worth a pound of cure. I'd walk a million miles for one of your smiles." Yeah! What are you gonna do with these expressions? If you ask me if you give the government 2.54 Cm's they'll take 1.06093 KM's![13]

Dale's conservative, concise, and critical comments are delivered with a wry humor – clearly he is a "provocateur who loves to stir the pot."[14]

HISTORY OF THE BARREL IN AMERICA

Figure 9-21. The cracker barrel scene – old men from an earlier time sitting around a pot-bellied stove solving the world's problems. The dog is unimpressed. From Michael and Vera Kraus, *Family Album for Americans* (New York: Ridge Press, 1961), page 78.

Today, recalling the words "cracker barrel" will likely conjure up in the minds of most the image of the Cracker Barrel Old Country Store ® and restaurant. Dan Evins, with the help of a friend, Tommy Lowe, started the business on September 19, 1969, opening the first restaurant and store in Lebanon, Tennessee. Today, there are 537 locations in forty-one states.[15]

Song Lyrics that Mention a Barrel

America still sings the praises of the barrel in lyrical verse. Perhaps the best known is Lew Brown's[16] 1934 composition *Beer Barrel Polka* with the chorus lines, "Roll out the barrel, We'll have a barrel of fun, Roll out the barrel, We'll got the blues on a run, Zing! Boom! Tarrel, ring out a song of good cheer, Now's the time to roll the barrel, For the gang's all here." Also the 1950 musical "Guys and Dolls" featured a song by Frank Loesser *A Bushel and a Peck* with

BARRELS: INTEGRATED INTO OUR CULTURE

the lyrics, "I love you a bushel and a peck, a bushel and a peck and a hug around the neck, Hug around the neck and a barrel and a heap, Barrel and a heap and I'm talking in my sleep about you . . ." A 1927 song written by Harry Wood titled *Side by Side* contained the lines, "Oh we ain't got a barrel of money, Maybe we're ragged and funny, But we travel along, singin' a song, Side by Side."

Aged in Barrels Today

Four products are still aged in barrels in the twenty-first century – wine (including honey-based mead), distilled spirits (see figure 9-22), Tabasco sauce, and several brands of Balsamic vinegar.[17]

Figure 9-22. A circa 1900 post card mailed to Eva Harrison in Henry, Illinois that E.L.M. is having a nice time in Summer, Missouri, and will be back home in few weeks.

HISTORY OF THE BARREL IN AMERICA

State Seals

After examining all the seals of the fifty states, only one, includes a barrel. The seal of West Virginia show a barrel adjacent to a miner and an anvil.

Figure 9-22. A black and white variation of the seal of West Virginia showing the founding date of June 20, 1863 on the rock, and a farmer with an ax to clear for planting, and a miner with a pick to dig ore.

Barrel Legend and Lore

With the millions of barrels in America, it seems there would be dozens of accounts about the container's role in ghost stories or in superstitions, but they have been difficult to uncover. Two are related below.

The Logger – Today, Cass, West Virginia, is a summertime tourist destination where visitors can take a short ride on the old Cass Railway that formerly hauled logs from the countryside into the small town. During 1992-93, Ms. Terry Stone worked in Cass as an interpreter of local history, taking visitors on a walking tour of the town and talking about such places as the 1901 general store and old jail. In her research for the assignment, she uncovered a ghost story about a logger, a barrel, and his ride to destiny.[18]

In its heyday, Cass was on both sides of the Greenbrier River, having a still-preserved section on the west bank owned and controlled by the lumber company, and on the east side a long-forgotten and disappeared portion comprised of homes, boarding houses, stores, saloons and brothels.

It was in one of these seedier establishments, frequented late at night by two-fisted lumbermen and ladies of the evening, that two men got into squabble. A short time later, one of them was on the floor dying. The other patrons must have disliked the survivor, who was herded outside, stuffed into an empty rain barrel, and rolled down the steep bank toward the river below.

Legend has it that his rolling, or perhaps barreling, down the side of the hill was not his undoing because he was heard screaming as the container disappeared into the night. When the barrel hit a tree, or perhaps a large rock, however, it shattered into pieces and his cries for help suddenly ceased.

He was found the next morning, killed instantly by a broken neck. A group of lumbermen dug a grave into the side of the hill not too far from the Greenbrier River where his bones are still interred. Some people claim that on a dark night when the moon rises slowly over the hill dimly illuminating the river valley below, his last screams can still be heard. Others say it's only the wind. We may never know.

Barreled Over – Another West Virginia incident about a barrel appears as a story titled, "Vinegar Hill" collected by Ruth Ann Musick. It seems several brothers lived on a hill and specialized in making cider vinegar. Musick writes, "One night, during a heavy thunderstorm, one of the brothers was going down the hill with a wagonload of barrels, the old mule stopped suddenly and the topmost barrel rolled off onto the driver, pinning him to the ground. His howls and groans soon brought his brothers to his aid . . ." but his rescuers, having imbibed too much liquor, pushed the barrel and let it roll with the unfortunate result, "The poor man was mashed twice as long as before." He was buried nearby, but at night his harrowing cries soon convinced his brothers to give up their vinegar-making business.[19]

HISTORY OF THE BARREL IN AMERICA

On a Less Serious Note

The policeman stopped a disheveled man going down the street clad only in a barrel. "Are you a poker player?" he asked. "No," the man replied, "but I just left some fellows who are."[20]

Many a boy wanted to be cooper like his dad or another role model in the community. Understanding this, Alfred Selwyn wrote a rhyming verse ending with a positive moral about a boy yearning to learn the trade.[21]

BARRELS: INTEGRATED INTO OUR CULTURE

THE JOLLY OLD COOPER.

A JOLLY old cooper am I,
    And I'm mending this tub, do you see?
The workmen are gone, and I am alone,
    And their tools are quite handy for me.
Now hammer and hammer away!
    This hoop I must fit to the tub:
One, two — but I wish it would stay —
    The workmen have gone to their grub.
How pleased they will be when they find
That I can do work to their mind!

HISTORY OF THE BARREL IN AMERICA

Yes, a jolly old cooper — But stop!
  What's this? Where's the tub? Oh, despair!
Knocked into a heap there it lies.
  To face them now, how shall I dare?
The knocks I have given the tub
  Will be echoed, I fear, on my head.
They are coming! Oh, yes! I can hear, —
  I can hear on the sidewalk a tread.
Shall I stay, and confess it was I?
Yes, that's better than telling a lie!

ALFRED SELWYN.

BARRELS: INTEGRATED INTO OUR CULTURE

The Final Words

Below is the epitaph of Thomas Hooper, cooper of Maynard Hill, Hamden County, Massachusetts.[22]

HERE LIE THE BONES OF THOM. HOOPER
WHO PLIED THE TRADE OF BARREL COOPER
HIS TOOLS WERE HOWEL, ADZ & SHAVE
HE FASHIONED HEADINGS, HOOPS & STAVE
FOR FLOUR BARRELS FOR THE MILLER
AND SPIRIT KEGS FOR THE DISTILLER
HE'D STILL BE AT HIS EARTHLY TASK
WERE HE AS SOUND AS WERE HIS CASKS.

FINIS.

[1] See http://memory.loc.gov/cgi-bin/ampage, Dec. 5, 2003, Alexander Hamilton, *Report on Manufactures,* 1791, p. 1000.
[2] As quoted in Robert E. Hardwicke, *The Oilman's Barrel* (Norman, OK: University of Oklahoma Press, 1956), p. 37.
[3] As quoted in ibid.
[4] Elizabeth Knowles, ed., *The Oxford Dictionary of Quotations* (Oxford: Oxford University Press, 1999), p. 305:23.
[5] The most frequently cited source is Christine Ammer, *The American Heritage Dictionary of Idioms* (Boston: Houghton Mifflin, 1992).
[6] Harold Wentworth and Stuart Berg Flexner, compilers, *The Pocket Dictionary of American Slang* (New York: Pocket Book, 1967).
[7] Gillian W. B. Bailey, "Cooperage," *The Chronicle of Early American Industries,* Sept 1950, 3:217, notes the Metropolitan Museum of Art in New York City has a drum "about the same shape as a barrel."
[8] Peter Matthews, ed., *The Guinness Book of Records,* 1994 (New York: Guinness Publishing), pp. 254, 256.
[9] William and Mary Morris, *Morris Dictionary of Words and Phrase Origins* (New York: HarperCollins, 1971).
[10] Wentworth, *Dictionary of American Slang.*
[11] H. L. Menchen, *A New Dictionary of Quotations* (New York: Alfred A. Knopf, 1991), p.153.
[12] For more on the cracker barrel, see the index in William Cahn, *Out of the Cracker Barrel* (New York: Simon and Schuster, 1969).
[13] Allan Dale, *Cracker Barrel Comments* (Wacko, TX: Texian Press, 1981), p. 45.
[14] Ibid, dust cover.
[15] See www.crackerbarrel.com, November 12, 2005
[16] Be*er Barrel Polka* was written by Lew Brown, Weadimir A. Timm and Jeromir Vejvoda.
[17] The author is indebted to Erwin M. Anselm of Front Royal, VA for pointing out that Balsamic vinegar is sometimes aged in barrels.
[18] The gist of the story was obtained from an interview with Ms. Terry Stone at the Mountain Made Gift Store in Thomas, WV on Oct. 17, 2004.
[19] Ruth Ann Musick, *The Telltale Lilac Bush and Other West Virginia Ghost Tales* (Lexington, KT: University Press of Kentucky, 1965), p. 81.
[20] As quoted from Jacob M. Braud, *Braud's Treasury of Wit and Humor* (Englewood Cliffs, NJ: Prentice-Hall, 1964), p. 27.
[21] Alfred Selwyn, "A Jolly Old Cooper," *The Nursery: A Monthly Magazine for Youngest Readers,* October 1877, pp. 123–24.
[22] Ellicott M. Sayward, *The Cooper and His Work,* 1969, p. 4.

Glossary

Barrel terminology and cooperage hand tools are defined and described in this glossary. To convey a better understanding, illustrations are included or in many cases the reader is referred to a figure in one of the preceding chapters. Names, spellings, and definitions vary with the country of origin, and the period, but here the focus is on American terminology during the nineteenth century. The shaded drawings are from Kenneth L. Cope, *American Cooperage Machinery and Tools* (Mendham, NJ: Astragal Press, 2003).[1]

Adz. A short-handled impact tool with a square hammer head on one end and a sharpened cutting blade on the other end. Used by a cooper for trimming wood.

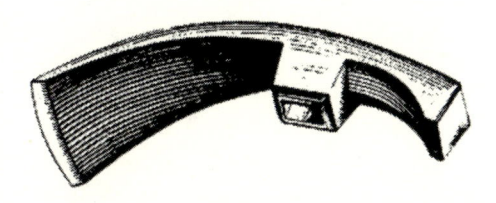

Figure 1.

Ax. A short-handled broad ax with an offset in the handle primarily used for trimming or listing staves. Also see figure 4-6.

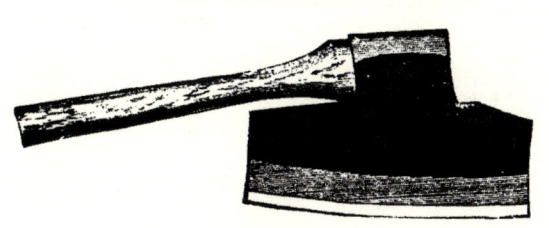

Figure 2.

Backing shave. A drawknife usually with a straight (but sometimes slightly curved) blade toward the operator used to shape the rounded back on a rough stave (see figure 4-9).

Barrel. A thin-walled cylinder with a bulging middle made of longitudinally tapered wooden slats of varying widths, called staves, each having slightly beveled edges that fit closely together and held in compression by strong outside hoops. The ends are fitted with

GLOSSARY

parallel circular discs called heads. Usually s*lack* (dry) barrels hold powders, soap, wax, and grains; and *tight* (wet) barrels hold liquids such as wine, beer, and whiskey. The main parts of a barrel are shown in figure 3.

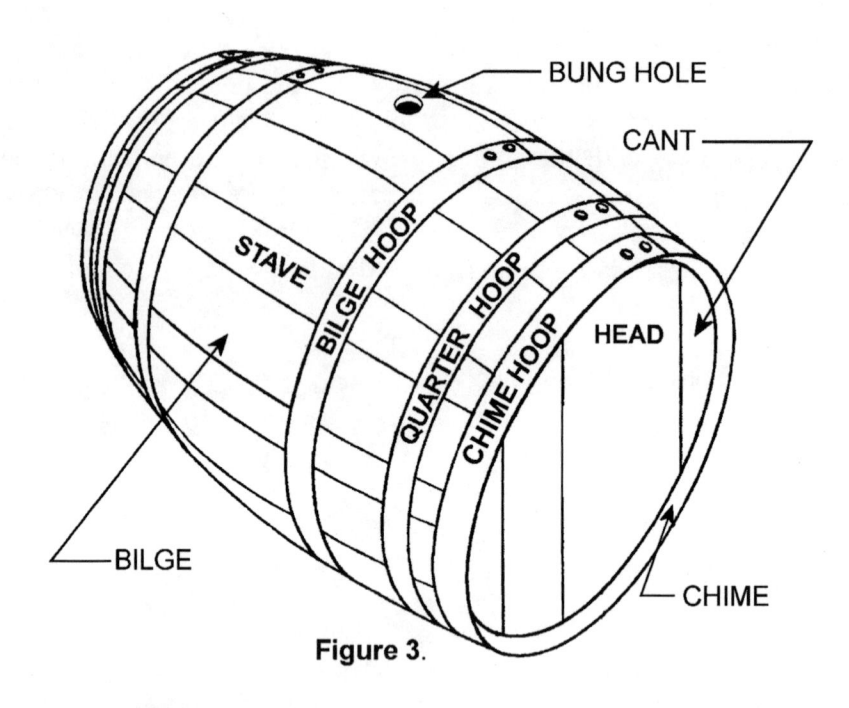

Figure 3.

Barrel heater. A small stove used to heat the inside of a headless barrel so the staves can be bent to the desired barrel shape (see figure 7-7). Also see *Cresset*.

Bead and bevel. The bead is the top or outside portion of the head. The bevel is both of the chamfered edges.

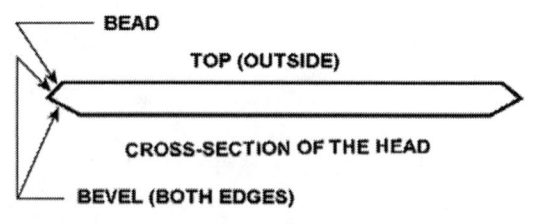

Figure 4.

Beakhorn or **Beak iron**. A cooper's anvil used in preparing metal hoops (see figure 4-25).

GLOSSARY

Bilge. The bulging portion of a barrel that is equidistant from each end, at the barrel's widest point (see figure 3).

Bolt. A section of a log (cylinder) cut to a length slightly longer than the required stave. (Also see quarter split.)

Bung. The plug inserted into the bunghole and used to seal the barrel after it is filled (see figure 3 and figure 2-15).

Bung borer. An auger, often tapered, used to bore the bunghole (see figure 4-27).

Bung starter. A wooden mallet with a flexible handle used to tap the bung stave to remove the bung (see figure 2-14).

Cant. In a multiple-piece barrelhead, the name given to the piece on the outside (see figure 3).

Case. A trussed barrel without heads. Compare gun.

Cask. In America, a name often applied to a large barrel. (Also see hogshead and keg.)

Chamfering knife. A type of drawknife used to cut the bevel on the edge of the inside of the staves to form the chime. Prior to the knife's introduction, it was cut with an adz. Also see figure 4-17.

Figure 5.

Chime. The inside chamfered edge of the top of the barrel that facilitates installation of the head (see figure 3).

GLOSSARY

Cresset. An open-ended cylinder made of strips of metal, which is filled with wood chips and lit from the top to heat the inside of a barrel, making the staves pliable enough to bend into shape (see figure 4-16).

Croze. The inside groove cut near the end of the staves, which provides a seat for the head. There were many variations as shown figure 6. Also see figures 4-20 and 7-8.

Figure 6.

Cylinder saw. A large rotating metal cylinder typically 18 to 24 inches wide (diameter) with saw teeth on the leading edge. It is used to cut staves having the approximate inside and outside diameter of the barrel. See an example made by the Peter Gerlach Company in figure 7-2.

Dowel pins. Short sections of small, usually round (but sometimes square), wooden rods used to hold the heading pieces together. See figure 7-11 and the text below.

Driver or drift. Used in conjunction with a hammer to drive hoops into place. See figure 4-26.

Froe or fromard. A cutting blade with an end-mounted, upright wooden handle. The back of the cutting edge is pounded with a wooden mallet to split or rive staves from a bolt. See figure 4-5.

Flag. A dried layer of a cattail used for caulking joints between staves or between the head and croze of a barrel (see figure 4-22).

Gun. An un-trussed barrel. Compare case.

GLOSSARY

Hammer. An impact device with a square head on one end and a chisel on the opposite end used to drive hoops on a barrel, pound rivets, and make adjustments to a barrel's shape.

Figure 7.

Heading float. A two-handed pull plane that is used for shaving the surface of a barrelhead flat and even.

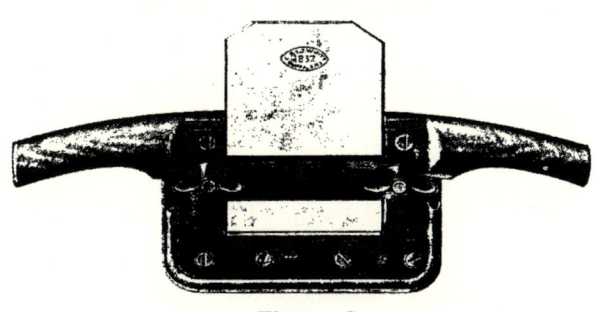

Figure 8.

Hogshead. In America, the name of a large barrel usually associated with tobacco.

Hollowing shave. A drawknife with a rounded cutting blade used to hollow out the back of a rough stave (see figure 4-10).

Hoop. An interlocked circular band of wood, riveted flat metal band, or twisted or welded loop of wire used to hold the staves of a barrel in compression. Depending on their location on the barrel, hoops have specific names of chime or head, quarter, and bilge (see figure 3). Generally, the quarter hoop is only used on tight barrels.

Hoop driver. See driver or drift.

GLOSSARY

Hooping-up. The process of placing and tightening the hoops on a barrel.

Howeling knife. Similar to a chamfering knife (see figure 5) but used to prepare the inside of the staves to an even surface prior to cutting the croze. Before the introduction of the howeling knife, a howel plane was used (see figure 4-19).

In-shave. Used to clean the inside of a barrel prior to installation of the heads. See figure 4-24 for two tools used to clean the inside of a barrel.

Joiner. A long block plane propped up on one end upside down and used to bevel the edges of a stave or join the edge of a piece for the head. See figure 4-13.

Keg. In America, the name applies to smaller barrels. The keg was often used to ship heavy items such as nails and railroad spikes.

Leveling plane. Also called a topping or sun plane, this curved device was used to level or even up the top edge of the barrel adjacent to the chime. See figure 4-18.

Quarter split. Riving a section of a bolt so the rough staves or blanks have the growth rings perpendicular to the split boards. See figures 4-4 and 4-5.

Scraper. Used to remove rough places from the inside and outside of a barrel (see figure 4-24).

Saw. A type of bucksaw, where rotating the vertical center spoke tightens the top line, thereby placing the blade in tension. The spoke is held in place by the center horizontal brace.

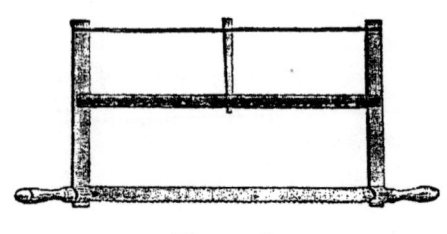

Figure 9.

GLOSSARY

Shook. A barrel knocked down into staves, hoops, and heads for shipping or storage.

Stave. One of the tapered slats that forms the outside of a barrel (see figure 3).

Sun or **topping plane**. See leveling plane.

Thief or vice. A metal tool with an oval handle and screw tip used to hold a head in place while installed in a barrel.

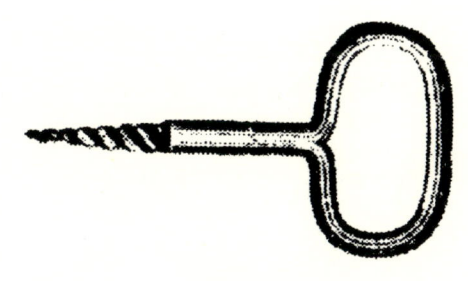

Figure 10.

Windlass. A hand-operated or mechanically-powered device that uses a rope or cable for pulling together staves so a hoop can be applied. See figures 5-17 and 7-6.

GLOSSARY

[1] Line drawings created by the author and engraved images from Kenneth L. Cope, *American Cooperage Machinery and Tools* (Mendhan, NJ: Astragal Press, 2003). The definitions are from multiple sources including the glossary found in Cope's book, pages 2–12, which in turn, relied on the *Wooden Barrel Manual*, 1951 edition, published by the Associated Cooperage Industries of America.

Appendix A

Products in Barrels and Kegs

Most every imaginable bulk product, either manufactured or agriculture, was shipped, stored, or aged in barrels or kegs. Smaller containers were used for heavy items such as the one hundred pound nail keg, while larger barrels were used mostly for agricultural products, such as apples and potatoes. Three principle sources were used for this list: Franklin E. Coyne, *The Development of Cooperage in the United States, 1620-1940* (Chicago: Lumber Buyers Publishing, 1940); *Chronicle of Early American Industries*, volume 44, page 107; and various issues of *Scientific American*, 1845-1900.

ale
applejack
apples, dried
apples, fresh
apricots
balsamic vinegar
beaver pelts
beeswax
beef
beer
beet sugar
biscuits
blackberries
bolts and nuts
bottles of wine
bourbon
brandy
brass foundry items
bread
brown sugar
butter

buttons
cane sugar
cement
cheese
chemicals
cherries
chinaware
chromic acid
cider
coal oil
cobalt ore
codfish
coffee
cognac
condensed milk
copper sulfate
corn
crabs, blue
crackers
cranberries
cream of tarter

crude oil
currents
dried fruit
dried peas
dry goods
earthenware
eels
eggs
embalming fluid
engine and machine
  oil
fertilizer
fish
flour
fruits
gin
glassware
gooseberries
grain
grass seed
gunpowder

APPENDIX A

hams
hard candy
hardtack
herring
honey
iron castings
ink
kerosene
lard
lettuce
lime
liquors
lobster
logan berries
meal
meat
molasses
mutton
nails
naval stores
oils
ore
oxalic acid
oysters
paint
pearl ash
petroleum
pewter
pickles
pilot bread
pork
porter
potable water
potassium
  bicarbonate
potassium chromate
potatoes
poultry

powdered glue
powdered milk
printer's ink
prunes
putty
railroad spikes
red raspberries
resin
rhubarb
rice
rosin
rum
rye whiskey
sal prenella
salt
salt mackerel
smoked shad
snuff
soap
sodium bicarbonate
sodium chromate
steam cylinder oil
stone
strawberries
sugar
syrup
Tabasco sauce
tallow
tar
terrapins,
  diamondback
tobacco
tools
turpentine
varnish
vegetables
vinegar
water

wax
whale oil
wheat
whiskey
white lead
wine
witch hazel
youngberries

Appendix B

Barrel Gauging

James I. Walsh notes that coopering was one of the most regulated industries in early America, so it may not be surprising to learn the various colonies, and later the states, passed legislation to establish standard sizes of casks.[1] Most often the London assize (an enactment that regulated weights and measures) was used as a guide in America so among the colonies there was a semblance of standardization.

Each colony, however, produced different products, which led to different container designations. In Virginia and Maryland, the tobacco cask, known as a hogshead, changed several times, getting as large a 1,250 pounds, but finally settling in 1789 on 1,000 pounds. In South Carolina, the rice barrel went from a capacity of 300 to 500 pounds, while Maryland and Pennsylvania adopted the London assize of 196 pounds for the flour barrel that was generally standardized throughout America.

In addition, the names of different size casks varied from location to location. Walsh[2] provides a representative table that includes: pipe, 126 gallons; tertian, 84 gallons; hogshead of wine 63; tierce, 42; beer/ale barrel, 34; barrel, 31-1/2; kilderlin, 15; and firkin, 8. There existed, however, much cask confusion, so inspectors used a variety of tools to determine the quantity of contents for tax and sale purposes (see figure 11B-1).

"In 1821 John Quincy Adams reported to Congress on the results of his state-by-state survey of the standards being applied to barrels and cask,"[3] but it was not until almost one hundred years later in 1912 and 1915 that the U. S. government finally standardized the size of a barrel, and then only for specific products (see table 5-2, page 115).

APPENDIX B

Figure 11B-1. Barrels came in many sizes and shapes so measuring them to determine the capacity was important. From J. L Nichols, *The Business Guide; or Safe Methods of Business* (Naperville, IL: J. L Nichols, 1902), page 337.

Over the years, there have been many rules and formulas derived or devised for determining the volume of a barrel, some more complicated than others. They are usually based on sound geometric principle of using an "averaged diameter" of the barrel. Eight of them are presented in table 11B-1. Using the dimensions for a U.S. federal government dry goods barrel established in 1915 with a volume of 7,056 cubic inches, each formula is evaluated. Specifically the barrel dimensions, in inches, from the regulations (see table 5-2) are:

H = 17.125 – head diameter,
L = 26 – spacing between heads, and
B = 19.87 – the inside diameter at the bilge. From the regulation the outside bilge circumference of 64 inches was divided by pi = 3.14159265, and twice the thickness of the staves (2 X 1/4 inch) was subtracted.

Figure 11B-2 shows graphically how the values are related to the dimensions of the barrel.

BARREL GAUGING

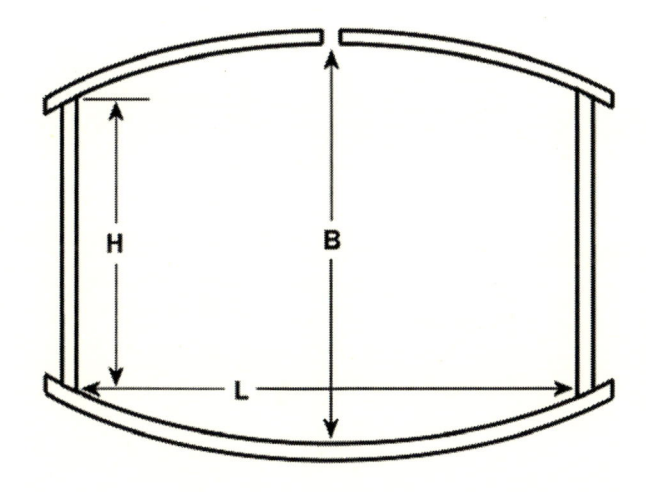

Figure 11B-2. Cross-section of a barrel with the critical dimensions labeled. Illustration by the author, 2004.

Table 11B-1. Comparison of the results using various formulas to calculate the volume of a standard 7,056 cubic inches barrel.

Formula	Source	Std. = 7056
$1/4\pi\, L\, [(B+H)/2]^2$	#1 Cooperage Handbook[4]	6987
$1/4\pi\, L\, [2/3B+1/3H]^2$	#2 Cooperage Handbook	7339
$1/4\pi\, L\, [2/3B^2+1/3H^2]$	#3 Cooperage Handbook	*7371*
$1/4\pi\, L\, [1/2(B^2+H^2) +1/10(B^2-H^2)]$	Everard's Rule[5] for spindles	7233
$1/4\pi\, L\, [1/2(B^2+H^2) +1/30(B^2-H^2)]$	Everard's Rule for conoids	**7097**
$1/4\pi\, L\, [1/2(B^2+H^2) +1/6(B^2-H^2)]$	Everard's Rule for cones	*7371*
$1/12\pi\, L\, (2B^2+H^2)$	Mark's Handbook[6] for circular staves (approx)	*7371*
$1/15\pi L\, (2B^2+BH+3/4\, H^2)$	Mark's Handbook for parabolic staves (exact)	7351

197

APPENDIX B

Everard's Rule for conoids produces the result of 7,095 (bolded), which is closest to the standard of 7,056 cubic inches. The least complicated formula, #1 from the Cooperage Handbook, produces a fairly close value albeit on the low side, a result benefiting neither the revenuer nor the seller. Note that three of the formulas produce exactly the same italicized value of 7,351 cubic inches. While not immediately obvious, the formulas are mathematically identical, with the one found in *Mark's Handbook* the easiest to use.

---

[1] James I. Walsh, "Capacity and Gauges Standards for Barrels and Casks of Early America," The Chronicle of the Early American Industries, 52:151–154.

[2] Ibid., p. 152.

[3] Ibid., p. 151.

[4] The Associated Cooperage Industries of America, *The Cooperage Handbook*, 1947 as found in Jim Packman, "Barrel Gauging," *The Chronicle of the Early American Industries*, 50:121.

[5] M. Dion and Edmund Stones, *The Construction and Principle Uses of Mathematical Instruments* (1758; reprint, Mendham, NJ: Astragal Press, 1995) as found in Jim Packman, "Barrel Gauging," *The Chronicle of the Early American Industries*, 50:121.

[6] Theodore Baumeister, ed., *Mechanical Engineers' Handbook* (New York: McGraw-Hill, 1958), p. 2-22.

Index

Adams, J. W., 130
Adams, John Quincy, 195
Adams, Robert F., 132
Advertising depicting barrels, 160–162
Adz, 80
Aged in barrels today, 177
Alden, John, 57
Ale in barrels, 119
Apple barrel, 114–115
Apple cider, 55–57
Backing shave, 74
Bailey, Ed, 150
Baltimore and Ohio Railroad, 95
Baltimore, 60, 91, 95, 161
Barrel and Box magazine, 38, 110
Barrel cactus, 168
Barrel chair, 169
Barrel distortion, 169
Barrel drum, 169
Barrel fever, 165
Barrel heater, 105, 141
Barrel jumping, 169
Barrel knot, 170
Barrel legend and lore, 178–179
Barrel leveler, 105
Barrel lot, 165–166
Barrel machinery, 104–107
Barrel of a baseball bat, 170–171
Barrel of a pen, 171
Barrel organ, 171
Barrel racing, 171
Barrel roll, 171
Barrel with accessible head, 121–124
Barrel, cleaning tools, 84
Barrel, comparison with wheel, 32–33
Barrel, competition from other containers, 116
Barrel, contents, 117–119, 193–194
Barrel, description, 27–28

Barrel, egg comparison, 34
Barrel, handling, 39–41
Barrel, heating, 79–80, 140–141
Barrel, invented? , 20–25
Barrel, making, 67–88, 135–154
Barrel, marking 146
Barrel, moving, 39–41, 124–126
Barrel, parts thereof, 69, 136, 186
Barrel, peak demand for, 96
Barrel, pre-stressed, 29–32
Barrel, production, 1906-1910, 159
Barrel, products in. See barrel, contents.
Barrel, raising, 77–78, 139–140
Barrel, robust, 27–43
Barrel, Shelburne Barrel Factory, 135–147
Barrel, size standardization of, 114–115, 195–198
Barrel, testing for leaks, 145
Barrel, volume calculation, 195–198
Barrel-chested, 172
Barrelheads, 82–83, 142–144
Barrelhouse music, 172
Barrelhouse, 172
Barreling down the road, 165
Barrels, integrated into culture, 159–183
Barrels, reproduction, 146
Barrels, special, 130–133
Barron, James, 173
Beak iron, 85
Beecher, Henry Ward, 11
Beef, 53–54
Beer Barrel Polka, 176
Beer, barrels of, 111–112
Beer, cooling, 129
Beni Hasan, 16
Benson, John, 99–100
Bible, 164
Billet. See stave.

INDEX

Blackbeard. See Edward Teach.
Bolt, 70–71, 135-136
Bottom of the barrel, 166
Bradford, Gov. William, 57
Bronze age, 14
Brooks Barrel Company, 149–157
Brooks, Paul, 9, 140–154
Brown, E.G., 98–99
Brown, William, 124
Bung, boring, 86–87
Bung, removing, 42–43
Burton, Elzy, 150
Butter making (churn), 126–128
Case, 80, 84
Cash on the barrelhead, 166
Chamfering and crozing machine, 107
Chesapeake and Delaware Canal, 95
Chesapeake and Ohio Canal, 95
Chesapeake, ship, 90
Chiv. See howel plane.
Cider. See apple cider.
Civil War, 100–103, 113
Clinton, Gov. DeWitt, 94
Clothing, 87
Cod fishing, 57–58
Compton, Erika, 9
Concrete, pre-stressed, 29
Conestoga wagon, 92
Cooper, Anna Julia, 173
Cooper, Dutch, 19
Cooper's anvil, 85
Cooper's block, 69–70, 73
Cooper's broad ax, 72
Cooper's clothing, 87
Cooper's joiner, 76
Cooperage industry, 115–117
Cooperage, indenture, 45
Cooperage. See slack, tight, and white.
Coopers, 107–109
Copper age, 14, 15
Country store, 117
Coyne, Franklin E., 9, 27–28, 52, 56, 63, 108, 115
Cracker barrel, 175–176

Cranberries barrel, 114–115
Cresset, 79–80
Curry, Dale, 173
Cylinder stave saw, 98, 137
Dale, Allan, 175
Dalley, William, 68
Damage tolerance, 28
Desire, ship, 58
Donleavy, J. P., 173
Dowels, 144
Drake, Col., 96
Drakeley & Fenton, 161
Drawknife. See backing shave, hollowing shave, and heading swift.
Driver or drift, 85–86
Dry goods barrel, 115
Eagan, Joseph, 9
Egyptian tapered tubs, 16
Eiselein, Adolph, 132
Embalming fluid in barrels, 119
Embargo Act, 90–91
Empty barrels make the most noise, 166
Erie Canal, 94
Evans, Oliver, 60
Fabyan, Robert, 165
Finch, Roy G., 94
Firkin, 195
Fishing in a barrel, 166
Flag caulking, 82, 145
Flatboats, 89
Fliege, Henry C., 124
Flour, 60–61, 91, 101, 109–111, 165
Footner, Geoffrey M., 94–95
Friederichs, John J., 124
Froe, 71
Fruit and dry commodities barrel, 114–115
Gage, Francis D., 174
Graham, Carlisle, 35
Grant, Ulysses S., 103
Hamilton Alexander, 159
Hamilton, Dr. Alexander, 56
Hanvey, Alexander, 122
Hays, Henry, 127

INDEX

Heading plane or swift, 84
Head-making machine, 99
Herodotus, 17
Hesy-re, 15
Hindle, Brook, 63
Hodsden, W. Wirt, 122
Hoerr, John, 129
Hoffman, John, 129
Hogshead, tobacco, 49–51, 195
Hollowing shave, 74
Holmes, E. & B. Co., 104, 107, 139–142
Holmes, Edward and Britain, 104
Hooper and hooper-cooper, 107
Hooper, Thomas, 183
Hoops, 142, 150–151
Hopkins, Gov. Stephen, 54
Howel plane, 81
Hyams, Edward, 17
Hyatt, Isaac U., 125
In the barrel, 166
Iron and steel age, 14
Jacobs, K. W. Cooperage Co., 109
Jefferson, Thomas, 89–90
Kentucky Fried Chicken, 174
Kernan, Mr., 102
Kilby, Kenneth, 9, 11, 15, 18, 32, 79
Kilby, Sam, 76
Kilderlin, 195
King James, view of tobacco, 47–48
Kirkland, Lane, 174
Knots, sealing, 141–142
Knox, Frank, 150, 152–153
Knox, Ken, 9, 155–157
Law, H., 97–98
Leach, Bobbie, 38
Lee, Robert E., 103
Leopard, ship, 90
Leveler for barrels, 105
Lewes, John, 45
Like shooting fish in a barrel, 166
Lincoln, Abraham, 101–100
Lindsey, G. W., 121
Listing a stave, 72–73
London assize, 54, 195
Loper, James, 59

Louisiana Purchase, 89
Lyrics. See song lyrics.
Maid of the Mist, barrel, 37
Marden, Luis, 34
Mark, John T., 127
Mess Pork hog medicine, 161
Mohawk and Hudson Railway, 96
Molasses, 54
More fun than a barrel of monkeys, 167
Mullins, Pricilla, 57
Music, Ruth Ann, 179
Native Americans, 12, 45–46, 61–62
Naval stores, 52–53
New Orleans, 89
Niagara Falls, 35–39
Non-intercourse Act, 91
Oil in barrels, 118
Oil, discovery of, 96
Oilstone, 87
Oliver, Francisco J., 123
Over a barrel, 167
Paint in barrels, 118
Peter, Rev. Hugh, 57–58
Pilgrims, 57
Pipe, 195
Pitch, 52–53
Pliny the elder, 17, 18
Pocahontas, 47
Population migration west, 91–93
Pork barrel, 172
Pork, 53–54
Port scenes with barrels, 162–164
Pre-stressed concrete, 29
Principio, 47
Products in barrels and kegs. See barrel, contents.
Railroads, 95–96
Raimondi, E J., 9, 44n
Rain barrel, 172
Reading Company bond, 162
Re-coopering, 43
Republican party, 174
Revolutionary War, 62
Rhuland, Raymond and Donna, 9, 135–147, photo, 147

201

INDEX

Rolfe, John, 47
Rotten apple spoils the barrel, 167
Rum, 54
Russell, Frank M. "Tussie," 35–36
Savidge, John, 59
Scheel, John H., 126
Scheetz, Marshall, 9, 76, 84, 85, 86,
Scrape the bottom of the barrel, 168
Selwyn, Alfred, 180
Seneca Chief, ship, 94
Shakespeare, William, 165
Sharpening stone, 87
Shaving horse, 75
Shelburne Barrel Factory, 135–147
Shepherd, E. W., 128
Shot or angle on stave, 75–77
Sisson, William T., 9, 71, 72, 73, 75, 78, 79, 81
Slack cooperage, 67–69
Soap making, 65
Song lyrics that mention a barrel, 176–177
Stansbury, James H., 125
Stave bucker, 99
Stave jointing machine, 98
Stave, cross-section, 141
Staves, 46–47, 70–77, 86, 136–138
Stone, Ms. Terry, 178
Strauss, S., 131
Sun plane. See topping plane.
Swift. See heading plane.
Tar, 52-53
Taylor, Annie Edson, 35–39
Taylor, Jim, 9
Teach, Edward, 55
Tertian, 195
The Jolly Old Cooper, 181–182
Tierce, 195
Tight cooperage, 67–69
Titusville, PA, 96
Tobacco, 47–51, 160, 162
Topping plane, 81
Townsend, Raymond, 9, 47, 53
Triangular trade, 54
Truesdale, Fred, 36
Trussing machine, 106

Turpentine, 52–53
USS Constellation, ship, 94–95
Vidal, Gore, 175
Virginia, Bank of the Commonwealth, 162
Volumetric efficiency, 116
Wagner, J. B., 96
Walsh, James I., 195
Washburn Crosby, 165
Washing cloths, 63
Well water, 64
West Bay Cooperage Co., 35
West Indies, 54, 58
West Virginia state seal, 178
Whale oil, 59
Wheat, 60
Wheel, 33
Whetstone, 87
Whiskey, barrels of, 110, 112–114
White cooperage, 67–69
White, Edie, 9
Whitney, Baxter D., 98
Windlass, 105, 139–140
Woodenware, 63–65
Wylie, Elinor, 175

202